Teddy Guinea Pigs

Teddy Guinea Pig Owners Manual.

Teddy Guinea pig care, handling, pros and cons, feeding, training and showing.
Ludwig Ledgerwood

By

Ludwig Ledgerwood

Table of Contents

5

About the Author

I have always loved animals but guinea pigs are by far my favorite. There is just something about the way they squeal in excitement when I enter the room and the way they jump for joy when I give them a pile of hay. That just warms my heart.

I have been keeping guinea pigs for more than a decade now and my love for them grows stronger each and every day. That is why I decided to write this book - to share my love for these wonderful creatures with you.

It is my hope that in reading this book you will come to understand why I love guinea pigs so much and that you might start to feel a little bit of that love yourself.

Introduction

When you hear the word "guinea pig," what do you picture? Perhaps you think of a small, furry creature that looks like a giant hamster. Guinea pigs are, in fact, very similar to hamsters in terms of their appearance but they are very different animals. Having kept both hamsters and guinea pigs as pets, I can personally say that guinea pigs are the better option. Although guinea pigs may be larger and require more space, they are definitely friendlier and more amenable to handling than hamsters usually are. They are also less likely to escape from their cage and to run loose in the house.

Guinea pigs make wonderful family pets and they are a great option as a first pet for children, as long as your children are old enough to care for them. Like all animals, guinea pigs do require some degree of care and attention, but they are by no means a high-maintenance pet. In fact, as long as you provide your guinea pig with a large-enough cage, a healthy diet, and lots of love, that is all they will ever really need.

There are thirteen different breeds of guinea pig, each with its own unique appearance. Some guinea pigs have short, coarse fur while others have long, silky fur. There are even some guinea pigs that have curly fur! This particular book is about a short-haired guinea pig breed – the Teddy guinea pig. The Teddy guinea pig is unique in appearance from other guinea pig breeds, known for having a dense, springy coat.

If you are interested in keeping guinea pigs as pets, the Teddy guinea pig is a beautiful animal and a wonderful pet. In this book you will find a wealth of information about the Teddy guinea pig as well as an extensive collection of facts and tips about keeping guinea pigs in general. By the time you finish this book you will have a thorough understanding of the Teddy guinea pig breed and you will be equipped to decide whether or not guinea pigs are the right pets for you.

So, if you are ready to learn everything there is to know about the Teddy guinea pig, keep reading!

Glossary of Terms

Below you will find a list of guinea pig terminology to help you understand Teddy guinea pigs and their care:

ACBA – American Cavy Breeders Association

Albino – A white-haired guinea pig with red (pink) eyes.

Alfalfa Hay – A type of grass hay that provides more protein and calcium than other hays; best for young guinea pigs; may cause obesity in older guinea pigs if overfed.

ARBA – The American Rabbit Breeders Association

Barbering – A condition in which the guinea pig chews it fur.

Bedding – The material used to line the bottom of a guinea pig's cage; helps to soak up moisture from urine.

Boar – A male guinea pig

Breed – A type of animal within a species that has a distinctive appearance; typically developed through selective breeding.

Caviary – A place where guinea pigs are kept and/or bred.

Cavy – Another name for guinea pigs; reference to the guinea pig's scientific name, *Cavia porcellus*.

Crest – A white whorl of fur on the forehead; seen in the White Crested guinea pig breed.

Fault – A term used in show to indicate a flaw that results in a deduction of points.

Gestation Period – The period following conception during which the pups develop inside the sow's womb; pregnancy; generally lasts 65 to 70 days.

Herbivore – An animal that eats only plant material.

Herd – A large group of guinea pigs, particularly guinea pigs living in the wild.

Litter – Referring to a group of pups all born at the same time.

Mane – Hair formation that grows long over the head and crown, then down the back; seen in the Silkie and Coronet breed.

Mange – A skin condition caused by burrowing mites that causes intense itching.

Nest Box – An enclosed space where guinea pigs like to hide and sleep; may or may not be used for breeding purposes.

Pellets – A type of commercial guinea pig diet typically consisting of dried hay pressed into pellet form.

Pododermatitis – Also known as bumble foot; an infection of the footpad that causes swelling and pain.

Popcorning – A unique behavior displayed by guinea pigs involving jumping, shaking the head, and squeaking; usually this behavior is an indication of joy.

Pup – A baby guinea pig.

Rosette – A whorl of hair seen in clusters or individually in a guinea pig's coat.

Rumble Strut – A behavior exhibited by male guinea pigs during mating; the male purrs vigorously while strutting around.

Ruttling – A rattling breathing sound that usually indicates respiratory infection in guinea pigs.

Sow – A female guinea pig.

Standard – A list of requirements for showing guinea pigs or for judging an individual breed.

Timothy Hay – A type of grass hay that forms the foundation of a guinea pig's diet.

Wheek – A high-pitched squeaking noise that guinea pigs make when calling attention to something.

Wraps – Or hair wrap; a technique used to care for the long coat of certain guinea pig breeds to keep it from dragging on the ground or from matting.

Chapter 1) What You Should Know About Guinea Pigs

Before getting into the details about the Teddy guinea pig breed, it would be beneficial for you to learn a little bit about guinea pigs in general. Guinea pigs are large rodents that generally weigh between 1.5 and 2.5 lbs. (700 to 1,200g). In this chapter you will learn the basics about guinea pigs including their history as food and pets. You will also receive an introduction into the many different breeds and colors for guinea pigs.

1. History of Guinea Pigs as Pets

The first domestication of guinea pigs happened around 5000 BC when the native South American tribes in the Andean region began keeping them for food. Statues of guinea pigs have been found in archaeological digs from Ecuador and Peru that date as far back as 500 BC and 500 AD. In fact, the ancient Moche people living in Peru worshipped animals including the guinea pig and these animals were frequently depicted in their art.

Around 1200 AD, selective breeding of the guinea pig began – this is when some of the first unique guinea pig breeds were developed. South American households kept guinea pigs in their homes, feeding them vegetable scraps, until they were fat enough to eat. Guinea pigs were also given as gifts in some cultures and, in others, they played a role in various religious and social ceremonies. Guinea pigs even played a part in ritual healing done by folk doctors – they were used to diagnose certain diseases including rheumatism, jaundice, typhus, and arthritis.
Guinea pigs continued to be used as a food source in South America for many years but when they reached Europe they became popular as exotic pets. Dutch, Spanish, and English traders were responsible for bringing guinea pigs to Europe – the earliest record of the guinea pig in Europe comes from 1547 in a description written by Santo Domingo. The guinea pig became a

fashionable pet among royalty and the upper classes – even Queen Elizabeth I had one!

The guinea pig was first scientifically described in 1554 by a Swiss naturalist named Conrad Gessner. Gessner is known for writing a 4,500-page encyclopedia of animals that he published in four volumes between 1551 and 1558. It wasn't until 1777, however, that the earliest binomial scientific name was given to the guinea pig. The scientific name *Cavia porcellus* is a combination of Peter Simon Pallas' generic designation given in 1766 and Linnaeus' specific conferall, which was given in 1758. The first artistic illustration of a guinea pig was made by an unknown artist in 1580 and shown in the National Portrait Gallery in London. This illustration shows a girl in Elizabethan dress holding a guinea pig with tortoise-shell coloration. This picture has been dated to the same time period of the oldest guinea pig remains found in England. These remains consisted of a partial skeleton found at Hill Hall in Essex, an Elizabethan manor house, and they were dated to 1575.

a. Naming of the Guinea Pig
The scientific name for the guinea pig is Cavia porcellus. The word *porcellus* is Latin, meaning "little pig", while the word *Cavia* is New Latin. Cavia is derived from the word *cabiai*, the name given to the species by the Galibi tribes that were once native to French Guiana. It is also possible that *cabiai* is an adaptation of the Portuguese word *cavia,* which comes from a word that means "rat". It is unclear how this species came to be given the "pig" name. It is true that they have a similar build to pigs, having a large head and rounded rump with no tail. In fact, some of the sounds the guinea pig makes are similar to the squeals of pigs. What is interesting is the fact that the species' name makes an allusion to pigs in a variety of European languages. For example, the German word for guinea pig is *Meerchseinchen,* which literally translates to "little sea pig".

The French word for guinea pig is *conchon d'Inde*, or Indian pig, and the Dutch refer to it as *Guinees biggetje*, or Guinean piglet.

The Chinese call these animals the "pig mouse" and the Japanese name is *morumotto*, which is the derivation of the name for another rodent, the marmot. It is also interesting to note that while most scientific references to the species use the name guinea pig, breeders of guinea pigs more commonly refer to the animals using a name derived from their scientific binomial name – cavy.

b. Guinea Pigs in the Wild

The domestic guinea pig, *Cavia porcellus*, is not found in the wild but this species is likely descendant from several closely related species like *Cavia fulgida*, *Cavia aperea*, and *Cavia tschudii*. These rodents are still very common in South America. There are also a few species of cavy that were identified during the 20th century – *Cavia guianae* and *Cavia anolaimae*, but they might be domesticated guinea pigs that were reintroduced into the wild and became feral.

Wild cavies are typically found in grassy areas, filling a similar ecological niche to cattle. These animals are very social, typically living in small groups that consist of a single boar and several sows as well as their young. Together, the group moves from one area to another, eating grass and other vegetation. Wild cavies do not build nests or burrow into the ground, but they do use the burrows made by other animals – they also use tunnels and crevices formed in the vegetation they feed on. Wild cavies tend to be the most active during the hours around dawn and dusk when predators are less likely to spot them.

2. Breeds of Guinea Pigs

According to the American Cavy Breeders Association (ACBA) there are thirteen different guinea pig breeds that have been currently recognized. These breeds are divided into three categories according to their coat types – smooth-coated, long-coated, and rough-coated. There are also two hairless/nearly hairless breeds that are not recognized by the ACBA – the Skinny Pig and the Baldwin. You will find a list of guinea pig breeds broken into their different categories below:

Smooth-Coated Breeds

This group of guinea pig breeds is named for their smooth, short coats. The coat should be consistently short in length and full with a smooth texture. It also has a good "fall", which means that it returns to normal after being brushed back. These include:

- American
- American Satin
- White Crested

Long-Coated Breeds

This group of guinea pig breeds is named for its long coat. The breed standards for these breeds require that the coat be of consistent quality. Guinea pigs that are shown in the long-coated category are divided into two categories – clipped and unclipped. Clipped guinea pigs are those that have had their coats trimmed at any point in time – once they have been clipped they will always belong to this category. Unclipped guinea pigs are usually pups or young adults and they are shown with their coat at maximum length and in full quality. These include:

- Coronet
- Peruvian
- Peruvian Satin
- Silkie
- Silkie Satin
- Texel

Rough-Coated Breeds

This group of guinea pig breeds exhibits a short coat with a rough texture in various colors and formations. These include:

- Abyssinian
- Abyssinian Satin
- Teddy
- Teddy Satin

Hairless Breeds

This group of guinea pigs exhibits genetic factors that render them hairless or nearly hairless. These guinea pig breeds require warmer accommodations as well as more energy-rich food to maintain their body temperatures. These include:

- Skinny Pig
- Baldwin

On the following pages you will find a detailed description of each breed of guinea pig.

American/American Satin

The American breed has a smooth, short coat and it is the most popular breed of guinea pig kept as a pet. These guinea pigs are generally very calm and they come in a variety of different colors. The American Satin is identical to the American in all ways except that its coat is finer in texture, more dense, and shiny. American Satin guinea pigs typically exhibit self-coloration while the American comes in nineteen colors recognized by the ACBA.

The American is the oldest breed of guinea pig, having been domesticated around 5000 BC. During the 1500s, when people began to selectively breed guinea pigs, this breed was originally known as the English guinea pig. In some countries it still carries that name, though the ACBA started calling it the American guinea pig in the 1960s.

White Crested

Also sometimes called the American Crested, the White Crested guinea pig breed is fairly rare. This breed was only recognized by the ACBA in 1974 and it does come in a Satin variety, though this variety is not recognized by the ACBA. The White Crested guinea pig comes in a wide variety of colors but all of them exhibit a crest of white fur on the head with no white on the rest of the body. The coat is short and smooth, like the American.

Coronet

The Coronet is a long-haired guinea pig breed that looks very similar to the Silkie breed. The main difference between the two is that the Coronet has a rosette, or coronet, in the middle of its head. This breed was developed from the White Crested breed

16

but, unlike the White Crested, the crest of hair on their head can be any color – this breed is also allowed to have white on other parts of the body. The Coronet breed can also be found in a satin variety, though this variety is not recognized by the ACBA.

Peruvian/Peruvian Satin
The Peruvian is a long-coated breed of guinea pig that requires a good bit of coat maintenance. This breed has long hair all over its body with a topcoat that can grow up to 2 feet long. The undercoat usually grows no longer than 7 inches and the hair parts naturally down the animal's spine. Peruvians must exhibit two rosettes on each side of the rump to be eligible for show and the hair should fan out from the body at such a length that it is difficult to tell the back from the front. The Peruvian Satin is similar in appearance but its coat is denser and has a glossy sheen to it. The Peruvian Satin is recognized as a separate breed by the ACBA.

Silkie/Silkie Satin
The Silkie guinea pig looks very similar to the Peruvian breed and it is a fairly new breed, having only been developed during the 1970s. The Silkie is the result of crossing the Peruvian with a self-colored black – it is known as the Sheltie in the UK. Silkie guinea pigs have slightly shorter hair compared to the Peruvian and it falls in a slightly different pattern. The Silkie's hair grows backwards from the neck, like a main, which leaves the face uncovered. The Silkie has slightly longer hair on the rump and, when viewed from above, it has a teardrop shape to it. This breed comes in many colors and the ACBA accepts all colors except tan for show.

Texel
The Texel is another easily identified breed of guinea pig, known for its curly tresses. This breed was only developed during the 1980s in England by crossing a Silkie with a Rex (this breed is not recognized by the ACBA). The Texel is similar in appearance to the Silkie but its hair is curled, instead of straight. The whole body of the Texel is covered in hair and there may be a natural

part down the center of the back. The hair on the face is shorter and this breed may or may not have longer curls along the lower jaw line and below the ears. This breed has a short body and a round, broad head shape. This breed is sometimes found in Satin varieties with a denser, shinier coat, but it is not recognized by the ACBA as a separate breed.

Abyssinian/Abyssinian Satin
The Abyssinian is one of the most distinctive guinea pig breeds, easily identified by their whorls of hair, called rosettes. This breed typically exhibits 8 to 10 whorls that frequently lie in specific locations. Abyssinian guinea pigs typically exhibit one whorl on each shoulder, one on each hip, four across the back, and two on the rump. An Abyssinian must have at least 8 rosettes in order to be eligible for show and the pattern must be symmetrical on the body. The hair of this breed is fairly short with a fine, silky texture and shiny appearance.

Teddy/Teddy Satin
The Teddy breed was developed as a result of a genetic mutation and it was recognized by the ACBA in 1978. Though once rare, the Teddy is now a very popular breed. This breed has a unique coat type that is short, dense, and fuzzy instead of smooth and silky. The Teddy has no rosettes and its coat is often referred to as being similar to the texture of a Brillo pad. This breed has a shorter coat than most guinea pig breeds and a Roman nose. There is a Satin version of the Teddy, which is recognized by the ACBA, but it is fairly uncommon.

Skinny Pig
The Skinny pig is a mostly hairless breed that is not currently recognized by the ACBA. Pups of this breed are born completely hairless but they develop some short, rough hairs on the feet and face. This breed was originally developed by crossing a hairless laboratory strain of guinea pig with the Teddy and other breeds.

Baldwin
The Baldwin is a nearly hairless breed of guinea pig that was developed from mutated American Crested pups. Pups of this breed are born with a full coat, which they shed as they age, leaving only a little hair on the feet.

3. Guinea Pig Colors

Guinea pigs come in a wide variety of colors and patterns. In all cases, the color is true – this means that the roots and tips are all of the same shade, except for ticked varieties. Guinea pigs colors are generally divided into three categories: self, ticked, and patterned. *You will find a description of each category and color listed below:*

Self
Self-colored guinea pigs exhibit a single, uniform color with no patterning or ticking. There are three different groups of self-colored guinea pigs: red series, black series, and white.

Black Self – This guinea pig has black skin with a black coat and black eyes.

Chocolate Self – This guinea pig has a deep brown coat with black skin and black eyes. The color may fade to steel grey or grey-brown in long-coated breeds.

Red Self – This guinea pig is reddish brown in color with black skin and black eyes – the coat should be as deeply red as possible.

White Self – This guinea pig is completely white in color with either clear red or black eyes. Guinea pigs with red eyes are referred to as pink-eyed white (PEW) and those with black eyes are dark-eyed white (DEW).

Patterned
There are ten different patterns for coloration in patterned guinea pigs – brindle, Dutch, Himalayan, magpie, tan, otter, fox, tortoiseshell, roan, and Dalmatian.

Brindle – This guinea pig has intermixed black- and red-series hairs throughout the coat with no ticking. In an ideal specimen, the coat appears to be uniformly colored with both black- and red-series colors evenly spread.

Dutch – This guinea pig has a specific combination of white markings. There is a white blaze on the face, a band around the neck and on the chest and belly – the front paws are also included as well as tips of white on the hind feet.

Himalayan – This guinea pig exhibits a white body with colored points on the face, ears and feet. The degree of darkness of the color points varies according to the temperature in which the guinea pig is kept. Himalayan colorations for show should have dark brown or black points with red eyes – the darkest color points should be on the face and feet.

Magpie – This guinea pig has a type of brindle coloration with black hairs intermixed for black-series and white hairs intermixed with the red series. This coloration is similar to the roan coloration but the white hairs can be anywhere.

Tan – This guinea pig is solid black with red ticking around the eyes, above the eyes, around the muzzle, under the neck, under the belly, and sparsely on the lower sides.

Otter – This guinea pig is solid black with yellow ticking.

Fox – This guinea pig is solid black with white ticking.

Tortoiseshell – This guinea pig exhibits patches of red and black color. Tortoiseshell guinea pigs raised for show should have well-defined patches of color as well as a seam on the back and belly.

Tortoiseshells with diluted colors are called broken and diluted tortoiseshell-and-white guinea pigs are tricolor.

Roan – This guinea pig has white hairs intermixed with colored hairs – both the head and rump are mostly colored.

Dalmatian – This guinea pig has colored spots on a white body and it is named after the Dalmatian dog - both the head and rump are mostly colored.

Ticked
Guinea pigs with a ticked coloration exhibit black hair with red ticking – this means that every individual hair has stripes of both red and black color. Ticked guinea pigs can exhibit a variety of patterns including tortoiseshell, agouti, and argente.

A guinea pig with agouti or argente coloring exhibits a solid-colored belly while the rest of the body is ticked. Ticked varieties with black or chocolate color and dark eyes are called agouti. Ticked varieties with grey, beige, or lilac color and red eyes are called argente.

There is also the possibility of a solid agouti or argente pattern in which the guinea pig is completely ticked. Ticked guinea pigs are named with the color first and the pattern second. For example, a guinea pig with solid beige and golden ticking would be called a golden solid argente guinea pig.

4. Guinea Pig Behavior

You may be surprised to learn that guinea pigs are fairly intelligent creatures. In laboratory tests, guinea pigs have demonstrated an ability to learn complex paths to food rewards and they are capable of remembering the path for several months at a time. Guinea pigs are not particularly agile and they do not climb well – they can, however, jump over small obstacles. These rodents are very skittish, starting easily, and like rabbits they either run for cover using darting motions when they sense a threat or they freeze in place. Groups of guinea pigs run in a scattered pattern when frightened as a means of confusing their predator and reducing their chances of being caught.

Guinea pigs are very social animals. In the wild, cavies typically live in small groups consisting of one male, several females, and their young. Domesticated guinea pigs are best kept in groups of two or more. Common combinations include groups of sows and groups of sows with a neutered boar. Guinea pigs participate in social grooming sometimes and they often groom themselves. As they groom, a milky white substance secretes from their eyes and they rub it into their hair. In some cases, groups of boars will chew on each other's hair when kept in groups – this is likely a method of establishing hierarchy, however, not a type of social grooming.

Male guinea pigs can be very violent with each other in order to establish dominance. They usually establish dominance by biting the ears of submissive males and by making aggressive noises and motions. Mounting behavior for dominance is also very common among same-sex groups of guinea pigs, especially for males. When a male tries to establish dominance he might make a rumbling sound – this is similar to the sound he makes when courting a female. When two guinea pigs are chasing each other they often make chutting and whining sounds – the pursuer chutting and the pursuee whining. Male guinea pigs often make chattering sounds by gnashing their teeth as a warning – they may also raise their heads in accompaniment of the sound.

Guinea pigs do not have well-developed sight like humans, but they do have a wider angle of vision and they see in partial color. These animals have very well developed senses of smell, touch, and hearing – vocalization is the primary form of communication for guinea pigs. Guinea pigs are sometimes regarded as a noisy pet because they are capable of making loud noises, but they are not constantly noisy. Generally speaking they only make noise when they want food or when males are fighting.

In addition to the sounds already described above, guinea pigs also use the following vocalizations:

Wheeking – This sound is similar to a whistle and it is expressed as a sign of excitement; it may occur in conjunction with feeding or the presence of the guinea pig's owner. Sometimes guinea pigs use this sound to find each other if they are running or lost.

Bubbling/Purring – Guinea pigs make this sound when they are enjoying themselves, like when they are being held or petted. They may also make this sound when investigating a new place or when grooming.

Squealing/Shrieking – This is a high-pitched sound indicating discontent and it is often made in response to danger or pain.

Chirping – This sound is less common, similar to a bird song, and it is usually related to stress. Baby guinea pigs may also make this sound when they want to be fed.

Domesticated guinea pigs can become very amenable to being picked up and handled as long as it is done from an early age. These animals seldom bite or scratch, though it does happen on occasion, especially if the animal is frightened. Guinea pigs are very curious animals, loving to explore new areas when they are allowed to investigate freely and when they feel familiar or safe with the area. One of the most unique behaviors guinea pigs demonstrate is called "popcorning". When a guinea pig is very happy or excited, he may jump in the air while shaking his head and squeaking. Guinea pigs also often develop a tendency to squeal in anticipation of food after learning that the rustling of plastic bags or opening the refrigerator door is a precursor to food being delivered.

5. Guinea Pig Biology

In addition to knowing the basics about guinea pig behavior, understanding guinea pig biology may also help you to be the best guinea pig owner you can be. Guinea pigs belong to the rodent family, which means that they are related to mice, rats, gerbils, and hamsters. Examples of wild rodents to which guinea pigs are related include dormice, squirrels, and capybaras. In fact, a capybara looks just like a giant guinea pig.

The physical characteristic shared between all rodents is their teeth, which are specially adapted to gnawing. A rodent's teeth continue to grow throughout its life so the animal must chew on things constantly to keep the teeth filed down. Different breeds of guinea pig are known for certain features. The Peruvian guinea pig, for example, is known for its long coat while the Teddy guinea pig is known for its dense, fuzzy coat. Some guinea pigs are born with no hair while others are born with hair but lose it over the course of several months after birth.

The digestive process guinea pigs go through is also very unique. When a guinea pig eats food, the nutrients pass through its digestive system and are excreted from the body in the form of soft droppings called "caecotrophs". The guinea pig eats these droppings directly from the body, thereby digesting the nutrients a second time so that as much nutrition is absorbed as possible. The second time the droppings are passed they are hard and pellet-like in shape. These are the droppings you will find scattered around your guinea pig's cage.

Not only do the guinea pig's teeth grow continuously, but so do its claws. In the wild, the guinea pig's claws are naturally worn down as they move across solid surfaces. Depending on what type of bedding you use in your guinea pig cage, your guinea pig's claws might not get worn down naturally. You need to check and trim your guinea pig's claws regularly to prevent them from becoming overgrown. Overgrown nails tend to curl and can actually grow back into the guinea pig's footpad, which can cause irritation and may lead to infection.

Chapter 2) Facts About Teddy Guinea Pigs

The Teddy guinea pig is one of the thirteen guinea pig breeds recognized by the ACBA and it is a very popular breed of guinea pig due to its unique coat. Teddy guinea pigs have short, springy fur and they come in a wide variety of different colors and patterns. Though you have already been introduced to this breed in the previous chapter, in this chapter you will learn about the Teddy guinea pig in greater detail. The information in this chapter will help you to decide whether the Teddy guinea pig might be the right pet for you.

1. Facts About Teddy Guinea Pigs

The Teddy guinea pig is a short-coated breed, also sometimes referred to as a rough-coated breed. These guinea pigs generally have thick, springy fur that doesn't curl like some guinea pig breeds including the Texel. The coat of the Teddy guinea pig is dense and kinky in texture. The hair is an even length all over the body and it is medium-length. This breed has no rosettes or ridges and the hair sticks out from the body. The short length of the Teddy guinea pig's coat makes it easy to groom and maintain.

The Teddy guinea pig is the result of a genetic mutation and it was first recognized as a separate breed in 1978. Although once rare, the Teddy guinea pig is now very common and they can often be found in pet stores. In addition to its short, springy coat the Teddy guinea pig has several other distinguishing features. This guinea pig often has a very thick, cobby body and it has an upturned nose known as a Roman nose. Other guinea pig breeds have flatter, narrower noses than the Teddy guinea pig but the American and the Teddy guinea pig breed both have Roman noses. This leads to some confusion between the two breeds.

In terms of temperament, the Teddy guinea pig is like most guinea pigs – it is typically very friendly and amenable to handling as long as you begin at an early age. The Teddy guinea

25

pig can be a little skittish when it comes to loud noises and sudden movement, but once they get used to being handled they will actually enjoy it. The Teddy is generally a healthy breed, however, like all guinea pigs, it is susceptible to certain diseases including diarrhea, scurvy, parasites, and respiratory tract infection. A healthy diet and clean conditions will help to ensure the health and wellbeing of your Teddy guinea pig.

Like all guinea pigs, the ideal diet for the Teddy guinea pig will consist of fresh grass hay and food pellets made from timothy hay. Fresh vegetables also play an important role in the Teddy guinea pig's diet and fresh fruit can be offered as an occasional treat. Fresh water is also very important for guinea pigs like the Teddy and should be offered in a water bottle that is cleaned daily. You will learn more about the ideal diet for guinea pigs later in this book.

Summary of Facts

Scientific Name: *Cavia porcellus*

Breed Name: Teddy

Size: 1.5 to 2.5 lbs. (700 to 1,200g)

Length: 8 to 10 inches (20 to 25 cm)

Lifespan: 4 to 5 years on average

Coat Maintenance: high

Coat Length: short, even length throughout

Coat Texture: dense, kinky and springy

Coat Formation: even length all over the body; stands out from the body

Rosettes: none

Coat Color: wide variety of patterns and colors accepted; self, agouti, solid, broken color, tortoise shell and white, any marked

Temperament: curious, friendly, alert, amenable to handling

Health: generally healthy; may be susceptible to diarrhea, scurvy, parasites, and respiratory tract infections

Diet: fresh grass hay and food pellets; fresh vegetables, fresh fruit on occasion; fresh water daily

2. How Many Should You Buy?

As you have already learned, guinea pigs are very social animals. Not only do they tend to live in groups in the wild, but they thrive best when kept in groups in captivity. This being the case, you should plan to purchase at least two Teddy guinea pigs or one Teddy and another guinea pig breed. Unlike some breeds, the Teddy guinea pig is easy to groom so it shouldn't be a problem to keep more than one guinea pig of this breed.

Guinea pigs usually get along well with each other unless you keep two or more intact males together. Intact males can be fairly violent with each other in the fight to establish dominance and the social hierarchy may change from time to time. The best way to ensure peace in your guinea pig group is to keep multiple sows together or, if you keep multiple sows with one boar, to have the boar neutered to prevent unwanted breeding.

It is possible to keep more than one male guinea pig together but you should expect a good bit of violence while the guinea pigs establish a hierarchy. Male guinea pigs tend to bite and claw at each other in their fight for dominance and the battle can get a little bloody. Guinea pig experts will tell you that if you want to keep more than one intact male guinea pig in the same cage that you will need to just let them fight it out. A little blood is unavoidable, but do not separate the guinea pigs except in the case of arterial bleeding. If you keep separating the guinea pigs when they fight and then put them back together, they will have to start the whole process over. Keeping multiple male guinea pigs in a very large cage will help to reduce fighting.

3. Can Guinea Pigs Be Kept with Other Pets?

Many new guinea pig owners wonder whether or not guinea pigs can be kept with other pets. Generally, the answer to this question is "no". Guinea pigs should not be kept in the same cage as other animals, even other rodents, except for maybe a dwarf rabbit that has a very mellow temperament. Because guinea pigs have different dietary needs than mice, hamsters, and rabbits, they should be caged separately. If you do choose to keep your guinea pig with a rabbit, try to separate them at mealtime so they each get the diet they need.

You may be surprised to learn that guinea pigs often get along very well with cats. You should always supervise interaction between your guinea pigs and other pets, but you may find that all of your pets get along.

The exception to this rule may be for terriers and other hunting breed dogs – dogs that were bred to hunt rodents or small game may view your guinea pigs as prey and chase them, even hurting them. Strangely, cats often enjoy guinea pigs and they may become great friends.

If you want to see how your Teddy guinea pig might get along with other pets you should enlist the help of a friend or family member. Have the other person hold onto your pet while you hold the guinea pig. Slowly move the two closer together until they are just a few inches apart and then gauge their reactions.

If your pet seems overly eager to get at the guinea pig or if he seems to view it as a prey animal, you should separate the two immediately. If your pet seems interested but not predatory you might be able to try an introduction in more open quarters.

4. Are Teddy Guinea Pigs Good for Children?

One of the most common questions new guinea pig owners ask is whether or not they are a good pet for children. Many parents choose a rodent like the guinea pig for their child's first pet because they can be kept in a cage and they are generally not difficult to care for. This is especially true for the Teddy guinea pig since it has a short coat that is easy to groom and maintain.

Teddy guinea pigs, and other guinea pig breeds, can be a good choice for children as long as you make the necessary preparations. Guinea pigs can easily be injured by mishandling, so you need to teach your child how to handle the guinea pig before you let him try. You should also make sure that your child understands the responsibility required in caring for a guinea pig and that he is capable of handling it.

Make sure your child understands that the guinea pig is fragile and teach him how to handle it properly. Guinea pigs are surprisingly heavy for their size and it is important that you support the belly and the bottom when you pick them up. Teach your child to pick the guinea pig up by placing one hand underneath it with the other hand supporting the rump – never hold the guinea pig so that its legs are dangling. After picking up the guinea pig you should hold it against your body or place it in your lap while sitting down. When it comes time to put the guinea pig back in his cage, hold him firmly to keep him from jumping out of your hands too early.

5. Ease and Cost of Care

Before you bring home a new pet, you need to make sure that you can provide for your pet's needs. For Teddy guinea pigs, this means providing a clean living environment, a healthy diet, and proper toys and cage accessories. Keeping a pet can be expensive, depending what kind of pet it is, and you shouldn't bring home a new pet unless you are confident in your ability to cover the necessary costs associated with pet ownership. In this section you will learn the basics about the costs associated with caring for Teddy guinea pigs including initial costs as well as recurring monthly costs.

a. Initial Costs

The initial costs associated with keeping Teddy guinea pigs include those costs that you must cover before bringing your guinea pig home. These costs include the cost of the cage, cage accessories, grooming supplies, and the guinea pig itself. *You will find an overview and estimate for each cost below:*

Guinea Pig – The cost of your guinea pig will vary depending on where you buy it. If you buy your guinea pig from a pet store, the price may be a little lower than if you purchase directly from a breeder. Costs will also vary depending on whether the animal was bred for show or as a pet. For the most part, you can expect to pay between $30 and $50 (£27 - £45) for a Teddy guinea pig.

Cage – The cost for your guinea pig cage will vary depending on its size and the materials you use. You may be able to purchase a guinea pig starter kit from a local pet store for around $50 to $75 – these kits come with the cage as well as some accessories like a food bowl, water bottle, and some kind of shelter. If you choose to build your own guinea pig cage or if you want a very large cage for a group of guinea pigs, your costs might be closer to $100 (£90) or more.

Cage Accessories – In addition to buying the guinea pig and his cage, you also need to provide certain cage accessories. These may include food bowls, water bottles, chew toys, and some kind of shelter. The cost for these items will vary depending on the quality and materials used, but you should expect to pay between $30 and $50 (£27 - £45) for cage accessories.

Grooming Supplies – Because the Teddy guinea pig has such a short coat, you will not need to do much grooming – occasional brushing should be sufficient. A small wire pin brush is the best tool to use in brushing your guinea pig. You may also want to invest in a pair of rodent nail clippers. The costs for these items will range from $25 to $50 (£22.50 - £45).

The chart below details the initial costs for keeping Teddy guinea pigs. Because it is recommended that you keep these animals in groups, you will find the costs for one, two, and three guinea pigs in the chart.

Initial Costs for Keeping Guinea Pigs			
Cost Type	**1 Guinea Pig**	**2 Guinea Pigs**	**3 Guinea Pigs**
Guinea Pig Purchase	$30 to $50 (£27 - £68)	$60 to $100 (£54 - £90)	$90 to $150 (£81 - £135)
Cage	$50 to $100 (£45 - £90)	$50 to $100 (£45 - £90)	$75 to $150 (£68 - £135)
Cage Accessories	$30 to $50 (£27 - £45)	$30 to $50 (£27 - £45)	$30 to $50 (£27 - £45)
Grooming Supplies	$25 to $50 (£23 - £45)	$25 to $50 (£23 - £45)	$25 to $50 (£23 - £45)
Total	$135 to $250 (£122 - £225)	$165 to $300 (£149 - £270)	$220 to $400 (£198 - £360)

**The costs provided above are intended for use as estimates only. Exchange rates for dollars and pounds may vary.

b. Monthly Costs

The monthly costs associated with keeping Teddy guinea pigs are those that occur on a recurring basis. Recurring monthly costs for keeping guinea pigs include costs for food, treats, bedding, nutritional supplements, and veterinary care. *You will find an overview and estimate for each cost below:*

Food – Guinea pigs are fairly small so they do not eat a lot of food at one time. Your food costs will vary depending how many guinea pigs you have and the quality of the food you feed them. Do not purchase food for your guinea pig based on cost or looks – the bright, colorful foods that may look best to you are actually full of artificial ingredients. The bland, plain-colored pellets made from timothy hay are actually what is best for your guinea pig. You should plan to spend about $5 to $10 (£4.50 - £9) per guinea pig per month on food.

Treats – You should not feed your guinea pig too many packaged treats, but fresh vegetables should be a part of his daily diet. You should budget for about ½ cup of fresh vegetables per day per guinea pig. You can also feed your guinea pig fresh fruit in very small amounts about once or twice a week. Because you can use vegetable and fruit scraps to feed your guinea pig, you do not necessarily need to spend a lot on fruits and vegetables. Plan to spend about $5 (£4.50) per month on treats per guinea pig.

Bedding – The type of bedding you choose for your guinea pig cage will determine the cost. If you use wood shavings as bedding you may incur costs up to $15 (£14) per month for bedding. If, however, you choose reusable bedding like fleece, you may only need to purchase the bedding once and just wash and reuse.

Nutritional Supplements – Guinea pigs will receive most of their nutrition from fresh hay, pellets, and vegetables but they may still require certain supplements. These animals are particularly prone to developing scurvy, which results from a deficiency in Vitamin C. To ensure that your guinea pigs don't get scurvy, you may want to dose their water with a vitamin C supplement – the cost for this is only around $5 (£4.50) a month.

Veterinary Care – Unlike dogs and cats, guinea pigs do not require vaccinations – they may not even need regular veterinary care. If your guinea pig gets sick, however, you might need to take him to a veterinarian who specializes in guinea pigs because not all veterinarians are trained for more than dogs and cats. The cost for a visit to a specialty vet is usually around $50. Two visits per year divided over twelve months results in a monthly cost of around $8.30 (£7.50).

The chart below details the monthly costs for keeping Teddy guinea pigs. Because it is recommended that you keep these animals in groups, you will find the costs for one, two, and three guinea pigs in the chart.

Monthly Costs for Keeping Guinea Pigs			
Cost Type	**1 Guinea Pig**	**2 Guinea Pigs**	**3 Guinea Pigs**
Food	$5 to $10 (£4.50 - £9)	$10 to $20 (£9 to £18)	$15 to $30 (£14 - £27)
Treats	$5 (£4.50)	$10 (£9)	$15 (£14)
Bedding	$15 (£14)	$15 (£14)	$15 (£14)
Nutritional Supplements	$5 (£4.50)	$5 (£4.50)	$5 (£4.50)
Veterinary Care	$8.30 (£7.50)	$17 (£15.30)	$25 (£22.50)
Total	$33.3 - $43.3 (£30 - £39)	$57 to $67 (£51 - £60)	$75 to $90 (£67.5 - £81)

**The costs provided above are intended for use as estimates only. Exchange rates for dollars and pounds may vary.

6. Pros and Cons of Teddy Guinea Pigs

Before you choose a pet and bring it home, you would be wise to learn as much as you can about it – this includes the good things and bad things about owning that pet. Teddy guinea pigs make wonderful pets, but they are not the right choice for everyone. Below you will find a list of pros and cons associated with Teddy guinea pigs to help you decide whether or not they are the right pet for you:

Pros for Teddy Guinea Pigs

- Teddy guinea pigs are very easy to groom and keep because they have a short coat
- Guinea pigs are very friendly animals that do not tend to bite or scratch.
- Keeping guinea pigs can be very entertaining due to their unique behaviors and vocalization.
- Guinea pigs that are handled regularly can become amenable to human interaction, even enjoying being held and petted.
- A guinea pig can be kept in a cage (as long as it is big enough), which cuts down on household mess.
- Initially, guinea pigs are fairly inexpensive to buy and to keep as household pets.

Cons for Teddy Guinea Pigs

- Guinea pigs require a good deal of space to ensure that they have room to exercise.
- Keeping just one guinea pig is not recommended – groups of two or more are better.
- Guinea pigs require regular handling and attention to keep them tame and amenable to handling.
- The guinea pig's cage must be cleaned regularly to maintain sanitary conditions.

- The costs for keeping a guinea pig can add up over time when you factor in recurring costs for food and bedding.

Chapter 3) Purchasing Teddy Guinea Pigs

In reading the previous two chapters you have learned the basics about guinea pigs as well as facts about the Teddy breed. Now that you understand the differences between the Teddy breed and other guinea pig breeds you should have a good idea whether or not this is the right breed for you. If you have decided that the Teddy guinea pig is the right pet for you, you are ready to move on to learning some of the practical aspects of buying and keeping guinea pigs as pets. In this chapter you will receive tips for finding Teddy guinea pigs, for choosing a reputable breeder, and for picking a healthy Silk Teddy guinea pig pup from a litter. You will also receive information about licensing and permit requirements for keeping guinea pigs as pets.

1. Where to Buy Teddy Guinea Pigs

Once you have decided that the Teddy guinea pig is the right pet for you, your next step is to figure out where to buy one. Purchasing an Teddy guinea pig may be as simple as stopping in to your local pet store, or it might not. Because the Teddy guinea pig a very popular breed it is a breed that many pet stores are likely to have in stock. If the pet store fails you, you can look for a local guinea pig breeder and see if they have any Teddy guinea pigs available. In the next section you will find a collection of tips for selecting a reputable guinea pig breeder.

Another option for finding a Teddy guinea pig is to check with your local guinea pig rescue. Adopting a guinea pig might be cheaper than purchasing from a breeder or pet store – you also have the benefit of talking to the person running the rescue about the individual temperaments of the guinea pigs available. Guinea pig rescues often have a mixture of adults and pups, so you might be able to choose whether you want an adult Teddy guinea pig or whether you want to raise a baby guinea pig. *If you think that adopting a guinea pig might be the right choice for you, check out some of the links for guinea pig rescues below:*

36

United States Gunea Pig Rescues

Metropolitan Guinea Pig Rescue.
www.mgpr.org/

Wheek Care Guinea Pig Rescue.
www.wheekcare.org/

Cavy Spirit.
www.cavyspirit.com/

Cavy Haven.
www.cavyhaven.org/

Peninsula Guinea Pig Rescue.
www.peninsulaguineapigrescue.com/

You can find more guinea pig rescues at the Guinea Lynx rescue list at this web address:
www.guinealynx.info/http://www.guin

United Kingdom Guinea Pig Rescues

Wheek and Squeak Guinea Pig Rescue.
wheekandsqueak.webs.com/

The Potteries Guinea Pig Rescue.
www.thepotteriesguineapigrescue.co.uk/

North East Guinea Pig Rescue.
www.northeastguineapigrescue.co.uk/

Blackberry Patch Guinea Pig Rescue.
www.blackberrypatch.co.uk/

April Lodge Guinea Pig Rescue.
www.aprillodge.co.uk/

You can find more guinea pig rescues at the Guinea Lynx rescue list at this web address: www.guinealynx.info/

2. Choosing a Reputable Breeder

The best tool you have at your disposal to find a guinea pig breeder is the Internet – you can perform a search to find local guinea pig breeders in your area. In order to ensure that you get a well bred, healthy guinea pig you should be very careful about the breeder you select. Perform a search to find several different breeders in your area and then take steps to evaluate each one, narrowing your list down to the best breeder.

In order to narrow down your list you will need to visit the breeder's website, call and speak to the breeder, and visit the caviary, if possible. Not all breeders will have their own website, especially if they only breed a few litters per year. If the breeder does have a website, look for pictures of the breeding stock, of available litters, and of the conditions in which the guinea pigs are kept.

The next step in your search for a reputable guinea pig breeder involves calling to speak to the breeders. When you call, make sure you talk to the person who actually does the breeding and runs the facility – you want to talk to someone who will be able to answer your questions. Ask the breeder questions about their experience with guinea pigs and, more specifically, about the Teddy guinea pig breed. Some breeders specialize in a particular breed while others work with several breeds. If the breeder works with several breeds you want to be sure that they have enough experience with the individual breeds to ensure high quality breeding stock and responsible breeding practices.

As you speak to the breeder, ask them questions about how long they have been breeding guinea pigs and what they do to make sure that their pups are healthy. A reputable breeder will have a good understanding of guinea pig genetics and will also put their breeding stock through some type of screening process to rule out hereditary conditions. The breeder should have no problem answering your questions – if he seems hesitant to answer your questions or is unable to answer them satisfactorily, cross them off the list and move on to the next option.

After you've narrowed down your list to a few different breeders, you may want to actually schedule a visit to the facilities. Seeing the conditions in which the breeding stock and the pups are kept will give you a good indication as to whether they are healthy or not. If the guinea pigs are kept in large, clean cages then they are more likely to be healthy than guinea pigs kept in cramped, unclean conditions. The breeder should have no qualms about showing you the breeding stock as well as the litters available. If you are satisfied with the conditions and the breeder's knowledge and experience, you can move on to actually selecting a guinea pig from one of the available litters.

To help you get started with your search for Teddy guinea pigs, check out some of the breeders listed below:

United States Guinea Pig Breeders

Teddy Bear Teddies.
www.teddybearteddies.com/

Rosewood Teddies.
www.rosewoodteddies.com/

Kristdala Kritters.
www.kkrabbits.com/

Charlotte Cavies.
www.charlottecavies.com/
You may also be able to find breeders through the ARBA breeder listing for rabbits and cavies:
www.arba.net/

United Kingdom Guinea Pig Breeders

Beauvale Cavies.
www.beauvalecavies.co.uk//babies-for-sale.html

Winterbourne Rabbits and Guinea Pigs.
www.winterbournerabbits.co.uk/

Longdown Activity Farm.
www.longdownfarm.co.uk/

K.L.C. Cavies.
www.klccavies.com/

Carrons Cavies Guinea Pig Boarding and Breeding.
www.carronscavies.co.uk/

Important Note: I have not purchased guinea pigs from all of these breeders. Make sure to check them out thoroughly before you buy from them.

3. How to Select a Healthy Guinea Pig

Before you actually pick out your guinea pig you need to take the time to familiarize yourself with the breed you are interested in so that you know what to look for. Teddy guinea pigs have long, flowing coats as adults but if you buy your guinea pig as a pup, the coat may still be fairly short. Still, you will be able to evaluate the guinea pig's general condition and the health of the coat, even if it is still short.

The first thing you should do when selecting a guinea pig is take a few minutes to just stand back and observe the guinea pigs. Watch them as they move about the cage, interact with each other, and respond to your presence. The guinea pigs should move easily without limping and they definitely shouldn't display any sluggish or lethargic behavior. If the guinea pigs have been properly handled and tamed they might still be a little skittish at sudden movements or loud noises, but they should not appear to be terrified of you. If you can, observe the guinea pigs eating as well so you can judge whether they have a healthy appetite – this is a good indication of health.

Next, examine the guinea pigs for obvious signs of illness or injury. The guinea pigs should have a healthy overall body composition – not too fat or too skinny. It can be difficult to tell the actual size of a Teddy guinea pig's body because its fur is so long, so you might want to actually pick each one up and judge its body composition by hand. You should also evaluate the condition of the guinea pig's coat. It may not be full-length if the guinea pig is young, but it should be smooth in texture and healthy in appearance.

After you've judged the general appearance of the guinea pigs, look for specific signs of illness. Check the guinea pig's eyes – they should be clear and bright with no discharge and no film over the eyes. The guinea pig's ears should be clean and free from odor or discharge – they should also be dry, as wet ears could be a breeding ground for bacteria. Check the guinea pig's teeth if it will let you – they should be well aligned and not overgrown. You should also check for wet or matted fur under the chin, as these are signs of problems in the mouth.

Next, check the guinea pig's breathing – it should be fairly quick but not labored. Place your ear near the guinea pig's face to check for gurgling or wheezing – these may both be an indication of respiratory infection. Check the guinea pig's rump to make sure there is no accumulated feces and that the anus is not plugged with fecal matter. If the guinea pig's cage is clean, this area should be fairly clean as well.

In addition to checking the guinea pig's physical wellbeing you should also handle it a little bit to judge its temperament. Well-socialized guinea pigs should be amenable to handling and they should not bite or scratch. If the guinea pig is still very young it might be a little skittish, but it should not appear panicked when

41

you hold it. Try petting the guinea pig gently to see how it reacts and check to make sure it is alert but calm, not lethargic or depressed. As long as the guinea pigs appear to be in good condition and good health you can feel good about bringing one of them home.

4. Do You Need a License?

When it comes to keeping Teddy guinea pigs as pets, the process is very different to keeping a cat or a dog. Still, you might be subject to certain licensing and permit requirements for your guinea pig depending on where you live. In this section, you will receive detailed information about licensing requirements for guinea pigs in the United States and the United Kingdom.

a. Licensing in the U.S.

In the United States, the US Department of Agriculture is responsible for administering and enforcing the Animal Welfare Act. The Animal Welfare Act was signed into law in 1966 and it is the only Federal law in the US that serves to regulate the treatment of animals. This act sets the minimum acceptable standard for the care of animals in research, transport, exhibition, and by dealers. Under the act, there are set standards with regards to handling, space requirements, shelter, watering, feeding, sanitation, ventilation, veterinary care and transport.

Under the Animal Welfare Act, the activity of certain classes of breeders and dealers of animals (including guinea pigs) as well as exhibitors and research facilities must obtain a license in order to legally engage in certain animal activities. In addition to obtaining a license, the entity must also submit to an inspection to ensure that the provisions of the Animal Welfare Act are being properly carried out.

The Animal Welfare Act does not regulate individual pet owners, most retail pet stores, and agricultural use of animals. This being the case, you will not need a license or permit in order to keep

Teddy guinea pigs as pets in the United States. The only exception is if you plan to breed your guinea pigs and you receive over $500 in gross income from sales in one calendar year. This only applies if you sell your guinea pigs to a pet store or dealer – hobby breeders do not require a license.

Even though you may not be required to obtain a license to legally keep Teddy guinea pigs as pets in the United States, you are still subject to meeting the requirements of the Animal Welfare Act in terms of cage and environmental regulations. *Under this act you must provide the following:*

- Minimum cage size of 10-by-10-by-7 inches for an adult guinea pig.
- Ambient temperature not below 60°F and not above 85°F.
- Fresh air by means of windows, doors, vents, or air conditioning to minimize odors, drafts, and moisture condensation.
- Ample light, by natural or artificial means, and both of good quality and well distributed.
- The cage should be placed so as to protect the guinea pigs from excessive illumination.
- Cage should be constructed of smooth material substantially impervious to liquids and moisture – no exposed wood.
- Guinea pigs should NOT be housed with any other species of animal.

b. Licensing in the U.K.

Licensing requirements for pet owners in the United Kingdom are a little different than they are in the US. You do not need a license to keep guinea pigs as pets in the UK – the only time you are likely to need a license is if you plan to transport your guinea pig into or out of the country. In this case you will need to obtain an Animal Moving License (AML) and you will need to follow certain procedures to ensure that your pet doesn't transmit any diseases during travel.

In the UK, pet shop owners may be required to obtain a license in addition to animal boarders. The animal boarding license requirements only apply to boarders of cats and dogs, however, not for guinea pigs, rabbits, hamsters, birds, reptiles, or other animals. Keepers of dangerous wild animals must also obtain a license according to the Dangerous Wild Animals Act of 1976. Unless one of these conditions applies to you, you will not need a license to keep Teddy guinea pigs in the UK.

Chapter 4) Setting Up Your Guinea Pig's Cage

While you may be able to give your Teddy guinea pig some time to play outside the cage, you should keep him in a cage most of the time to keep him safe. There is no rule, however, stating that you must keep him in a certain type of cage. Guinea pigs are active animals that require a good bit of space to run around – if you keep your Teddy guinea pig in a cage that is too small, he may fail to thrive. Cage size is especially important if you plan to keep more than one guinea pig together. In this chapter you will learn the basics about habitat requirements for guinea pigs and you will receive some tips for setting up your Teddy guinea pig's cage. You will also receive information about building a custom guinea pig cage from scratch and ideas for different types of bedding. By the time you finish this chapter you will be ready to create the ultimate living space for your Teddy guinea pig to ensure that he stays happy and healthy in your care.

1. Habitat Requirements

Domesticated guinea pigs like the Teddy guinea pig spend almost their entire lives in their cages, so it is very important that your guinea pig's cage provides for his basic needs. When it comes to setting up your guinea pig's cage you need to think about things like cage size, cage material, and cage location. *Below you will find an overview of the requirements for each of these categories:*

Cage Size
The size of your Teddy guinea pig's cage will vary depending on how many other guinea pigs you keep with him. For one to two guinea pigs, a minimum cage size of 40 inches long by 20 inches wide by 20 inches high (102x51x51 cm) is recommended. If you follow the recommendations of the Humane Society of the United States, however, you will find slightly different recommendations, which are listed below:

One guinea pig – about 30-by-36 inches (76x91 cm); about 7.5 square feet (2.3m) of space

Two guinea pigs – about 30-by-50 inches (76x127 cm); about 10.5 square feet (3.2m) of space

Three guinea pigs – about 30-by-62 inches (76x157 cm); about 13 square feet (4m) of space

Four guinea pigs – about 30-by-76 inches (76x193 cm); minimum of 13 square feet (4m) of space

When in doubt, it is always better to go with a larger cage than a smaller cage. Larger cages provide your guinea pig with adequate room to exercise, which can help reduce their risk for developing medical problems. In addition, consider the fact that your guinea pig will spend its entire 5- to 7-year life in its cage, you can see how a little extra space might be important. Furthermore, large cages are easier to clean because waste won't buildup in one particular area. For male guinea pigs, a large cage can make the difference between daily duels and peaceful coexistence.

Referring back to the provisions of the Animal Welfare Act, only 10x10x7 inches (25.4x25.4x18 cm) of space per guinea pig is required. These recommendations are intended to indicate the bare minimum requirements for survival of the species, however – this amount of space only gives the guinea pig room to "make normal postural adjustments with adequate freedom of movement". A cage this small becomes little more than a litter box for your guinea pig, however, so it is important that you exceed these minimum requirements and exceed them significantly for your guinea pig's benefit.

Cage Material
According to the Animal Welfare Act, a guinea pig cage should be composed of "smooth material substantially impervious to liquids and moisture". Given these requirements you might think

that glass aquariums make good guinea pig cages because they are impervious to moisture. In reality, a glass cage is the worst thing you can do for your guinea pig because it holds in too much heat and humidity. You should also avoid rabbit cages and other cages that have wire bottoms because they will irritate your guinea pig's feet.

The best cage materials are plastic and metal. Ideally, your guinea pig cage should have a plastic bottom with sides constructed from metal mesh or wire. The plastic bottom will prevent leaking and it will contain your guinea pig's bedding. With wire mesh walls, your guinea pig will enjoy plenty of fresh air and good ventilation to reduce odor and moisture accumulation. You can find cages like this at most retail pet stores and online – you can also build them yourself by following the instructions provided later in this chapter. DIY guinea pig cages are preferred by most serious cavy enthusiasts because you have the ability to customize your cage dimensions to make sure you have enough space for the number of guinea pigs you have. They are also surprisingly easy to build if you have the right materials.

Cage Location
The third factor that comes into consideration for guinea pig habitat requirements is cage location. The following list will give you an idea of what you need to consider when choosing a location for your Teddy guinea pig cage:

Light – In the wild, guinea pigs are the most active during dawn and dusk hours. In captivity, however, they can be active at any time of day – most of the time, they nap for a few hours then wake up to eat and move around. Guinea pigs do not have any biological requirement for natural light, but you should still provide your guinea pigs with adequate lighting. The ideal location will be a room that is brightly lit by indirect sunlight. You can also place your cage under a window that gets morning light only – too much direct sunlight could affect temperatures in your guinea pig cage.

Temperature – The ideal temperature range for guinea pigs is between 65°F and 75°F (18°C to 24°C). Guinea pigs should not be kept in temperatures below 60°F (15.5°C) and they are likely to suffer from heat stroke in temperatures above 85°F (29°C). A general rule to follow is that if you are comfortable at the temperature, your guinea pigs probably will be too.

Humidity – The ideal location for your guinea pig cage will have a low, stable humidity level. Areas that are close to showers, laundry rooms, and in finished basements tend to have higher humidity levels that can be bad for guinea pigs. On the opposite end of the spectrum, you should also avoid areas that are too drafty such as areas next to cooling vents, next to windows, or near doors to the outside. Guinea pigs are very susceptible to respiratory infections so they should not be exposed to drafts.

Proximity – The final factor to consider when choosing a location for your guinea pig cage is proximity to people. For the long-term health and happiness of your guinea pig, you should keep the cage in a location where there is some family activity. The best location is near the kitchen or family room – these are locations where your family spends the most time. When you keep your guinea pigs nearby you can more easily monitor their behavior and interact with them more regularly.

In addition to considering these requirements for your guinea pig's cage location you should also think about some things that you need to avoid. Do not keep your guinea pig cage on the floor, for example. If you do, your guinea pigs could be easily scared by you since you will appear like a giant to them. Movement, vacuuming, cleaning, and other activities that produce noise will be more stressful for your guinea pigs if they are on the floor. In addition, guinea pigs are not as easy to pet and interact with if they are on the floor.

Another important thing to consider in terms of guinea pig habitat requirements is whether you keep them indoors or outdoors. The most important factor to think about is temperature – if you live in a climate that matches the ideal temperature range for your guinea pigs, keeping them in an outdoor hutch might be a viable option. The downside of keeping your guinea pigs outdoors is that you will spend less time interacting with them and they may be more likely to contract disease, especially if they come into contact with a wild animal. In general, guinea pigs kept indoors live longer lives than those kept outdoors.

2. Types of Cages

When it comes to choosing a type of cage for your Teddy guinea pig, you have several options. Below you will find an overview of the most common guinea pig cage types as well as some pros and cons for each:

Glass/Acrylic Aquarium – As you have already learned, it is never recommended that you keep your guinea pig in a glass or acrylic aquarium. Unfortunately, many people still do not know or understand the dangers of keeping a guinea pig in this type of cage. While aquariums are an inexpensive option and easy to clean, they do not get much air circulation and most of them are too small for even a single guinea pig to be happy.

Pet Store Cage – Pet stores sell guinea pig cages in a variety of sizes, mostly with plastic bottoms and a wire mesh cage around the sides and over the top. These cages appeal to new guinea pig owners because they often come with additional accessories like food bowls, water bottles, and even food. While this option may be cost-effective and easy, many commercial cages do not offer enough space for more than one guinea pig. If you choose to go with a pet store cage, make sure it meets the minimum cage size recommendations outlined in the previous section.

Outdoor Hutch – An outdoor hutch is typically used for rabbits, but some cavy enthusiasts use them for guinea pigs. The only time you should keep your guinea pigs outside in a hutch is when the climate in your area matches the temperature requirements for guinea pigs. You also need to consider the fact that many outdoor hutches are made from wood – this material tends to absorb moisture and it might foster bacteria and fungus unless it is sealed and cleaned regularly. Keeping your guinea pig in an outdoor hutch may be more work than you want to do.

Cubes and Coroplast – The most popular type of cage for guinea pigs is the cubes and coroplast, or C&C cage. These cages consist of a cage base made from corrugated plastic (coroplast) and a frame made from square wire mesh grids. There are a few websites where you can go to order custom C&C cages or to purchase a kit to build your own. You can also purchase the materials and build the cage yourself to whatever dimensions you like. You will find detailed instructions for building a C&C guinea pig cage later in this chapter.

Other – Though aquariums, pet store cages, hutches, and C&C cages are the most popular options for guinea pig housing, some guinea pig owners get creative. You could build a playpen for your guinea pigs using a child's swimming pool or a puppy playpen lined with old towels. Feel free to make a guinea pig cage out of unconventional materials as long as it adheres to the size requirements listed earlier.

3. Recommended Cage Accessories

In addition to providing your Teddy guinea pig with a clean and safe habitat, you also need to provide a few cage accessories. The most important accessories to have for a guinea pig cage are food bowls, water bottle, chew toys, and some type of shelter. You will find an overview of these cage accessories below:

Food Bowl – Depending on the number of guinea pigs you plan to keep in your cage, you may need more than one food bowl. The most important things to consider when choosing food bowls for your guinea pig cage is access and sanitation. The sides of the bowl should not be so high that your guinea pig can't easily access the food, but they shouldn't be so low that the guinea pig can easily tip the bowl over. In terms of materials, ceramic dishes are a popular choice because they come in a variety of colors and they are easy to clean and sanitize. Plastic bowls will become chew toys for your guinea pigs and they might harbor bacteria in the scratches left by sharp guinea pig teeth.

Water Bottle – Guinea pigs need constant access to fresh water so you should equip your cage with one water bottle for every two guinea pigs. When placing the water bottle, hang it on the outside of the cage with the nozzle poking through the side of the cage – guinea pigs will chew on bottles that are hung inside the cage. In addition to keeping the water bottle full, you should also clean it on a daily basis because the inside will become slimy and they could harbor dangerous bacteria. You can clean the bottle with a mild bleach solution and rinse it very well before refilling and hanging it.

Chew Toys – Provide your guinea pig with several types of toys to provide them with mental and physical stimulation. Chew toys should be made from wood (untreated) – you can also use untreated branches from fruit trees to give your guinea pig something to chew on to keep his teeth from becoming overgrown. Guinea pigs also enjoy chewing on paper towel tubes and cardboard boxes. Guinea pigs do not play with toys in the same way that dogs or cats do, though some of them will play with things like plastic cups, wooden blocks, and similar objects. The most important toys for guinea pigs, however, are chew toys to help wear down their teeth.

Shelter – Guinea pigs will sleep out in the open if they feel comfortable but many prefer to sleep inside some type of shelter. At the very least, provide your guinea pigs with a cardboard box to hide in. You can also find wood or plastic hide houses at the pet store or online. Make sure you add enough hide houses in your guinea pig cage so that each of your guinea pigs can use one at the same time if they want to.

Additional Accessories – Many guinea pig enthusiasts like to make their own guinea pig accessories. Fleece is a versatile material that can be used to make hammocks, sleeping bags, and tunnels for guinea pigs. If you aren't crafty yourself, you can find handmade guinea pig accessories on eBay or Etsy. If you want to try your hand at making DIY guinea pig accessories, you can find them on Pinterest.

Bedding – While not technically a cage accessory, bedding is an important part of the guinea pig cage. Lining the bottom of your guinea pig's cage with some type of bedding will help to absorb moisture and to keep your guinea pig clean. Some of the most popular types of bedding include wood shavings, recycled paper bedding, fresh hay, and fleece. Wood shavings are one of the least expensive options and it is easy to use – just spread about 3 inches of it on the bottom of your guinea pig's cage and change it out once a week. Recycled paper bedding is a little more expensive but it absorbs moisture well and comes in a variety of colors. Fresh hay is great bedding because your guinea pig can eat it, but you need to change it out frequently to keep it fresh. Fleece is a great option because it is reusable but you will need to line the bottom of the cage with some liquid-absorbing material and wash the fleece every week to keep it clean.

4. Building Your Own C&C Cage

If you want to build your own cage for your Teddy guinea pig, your best option is a cubes and coroplast, or C&C cage. This type of cage is fairly easy to assemble and it is very cost-effective as well. Once you assemble the cage you have the option to whatever kind of bedding you like – wood shavings, recycled paper bedding, fresh hay, or fleece.

There are some challenges associated with the C&C cage but, for the most part, the benefits outweigh the negatives. Below you will find a list of pros and cons for the C&C cage:

Pros for C&C Cages

- Can be built with whatever cage dimensions you like.
- Easy to build and easy to make changes to the design.

- Comes in a variety of different color choices.
- Great way to maximize space in the home.
- Aesthetically pleasing, especially when paired with fleece lining.
- Very durable and offers excellent air circulation.
- Gives you the ability to add levels.
- Can be cat-proof by adding a top to the cage.
- Lightweight; can be used on top of folding tables for support.
- Collapsible for easy storage or transport.

Cons for C&C Cages

- Materials may not be available in pet stores – can be hard to find.
- Sources for coroplast are limited.
- Large sheets of coroplast can be difficult to transport.

Before you learn how to build a C&C cage you need to understand what the materials are that you will be using. The two main materials are sheets of corrugated plastic (coroplast) and 14-inch coated-wire grid – the kind used to build storage cubes. You will also need the plastic connectors that come with a set of storage cubes or an assortment of cable ties (zip ties). You can find cable ties at your local hardware store and sets of storage cubes online or in stores that carry home goods like Walmart, Kmart, Target, Linens N' Things, Bed Bath and Beyond, and more. For coroplast, you may need to find a local sign store – the type of store that makes signs for businesses.

In addition to the materials needed for a C&C cage, you should also familiarize yourself with the different styles:

Open Cage – This type of cage is built with a single level and an open top.

Closed Cage – This type of cage is built with a single level and the grids go all the way around the sides and over the top, usually to keep out dogs and cats.

Open Two-Level Cage – This type of cage has sections at two different levels, both with an open top – it is common to use a large bottom level with a ramp up to a smaller second-level deck.

Closed Two-Level Cage – This type of cage has closed sections at two different levels to keep out dogs and cats.

Now that you know the basics about what a C&C cage looks like and how it is composed you are ready to learn how to build one yourself.

Follow the instructions below to build your own C&C cage for your Teddy guinea pig:

1. Determine the minimum cage dimensions for your cage using the information from the previous section – the cage size will be determined by the number of guinea pigs you keep.

2. Assemble your materials so they are within easy reach – you will need one or two sets of coated wire grids, the included plastic connectors, plastic cable ties, and a large sheet of coroplast. You will also need scissors or a utility knife.

3. Assemble the perimeter of the cage (the frame) using the coated wire grids and the included connectors – measure to make sure it meets the minimum cage dimension requirements and remember that it is better to go bigger than smaller.

4. Measure the length and width of the enclosure on the inside of the grids – most grids measure 14-by-14 inches (35.5x35.5cm) with some additional space added for the

plastic connectors.

5. Add twelve inches to the length and width measurements you just took – this will account for a 6-inch (15.2cm) wall all the way around the inside of the cage to contain bedding.

6. Measure and mark your sheet of coroplast using the dimensions you just measured – cut it to size.

7. Draw lines across the length and width of the coroplast 6 inches in from each side and score the lines using the utility knife (be careful not to cut all the way through).

8. Cut 6 inches in through the coroplast at each corner to create a flap at each corner.

9. Snap the edges along the scored lines, folding them up toward the center.

10. Overlap the corner flaps and secure them in place using clear packing tape on the outside of the frame.

11. Place the coroplast box inside the wire grid frame.

12. Fill it with your choice of bedding, add your cage accessories, then let your guinea pigs run free in their brand new home.

Building your own guinea pig cage is that easy – all you need is a few simple materials and a little bit of time. Feel free to get creative with your design, adding a ramp to a second level or taping multiple pieces of coroplast together to make an L-shaped rather than a rectangular cage. The options are limited only by your imagination.

5. Guinea Pig Cage Maintenance

After you have taken the time to set up your guinea pig cage and let your guinea pigs loose, all that you have to do is maintain proper cleanliness and sanitation in the cage. Guinea pig cage maintenance involves refreshing the bedding as needed, cleaning food and water containers, and cleaning the cage. Below you will find a list of maintenance tasks divided into categories by daily and weekly requirements:

Daily Cage Maintenance

- Spot clean the cage, removing soiled bedding
- Clean the water bottle with a mild bleach solution and refill
- Sanitize the food bowls and refill
- Check for chew toys or other cage accessories that need to be replaced

Weekly Cage Maintenance

- Remove and replace all of the bedding
- Wipe down the interior of the cage with mild dish soap and warm water
- Wipe down the cage with a milk bleach and water solution (mix at a ratio of 1:32)
- Scrub all cage furniture clean with the same bleach solution
- Rinse all surfaces well with warm water

Chapter 5) Feeding Your Teddy Guinea Pig

As is true for any pet, feeding your Teddy guinea pig a healthy diet will have a direct impact on his health and wellbeing. If you do not offer your guinea pig a healthy diet, he cannot possibly be healthy – it is as simple as that. You may save some money in the short term by buying a low-quality food, but you may end up spending more on vet fees in the long term. Feeding your Teddy guinea pig involves more than just throwing some vegetables into the cage or filling his bowl with food pellets. Like all animals, guinea pigs require a certain balance of nutrients in order to maintain their good health. Feeding your Teddy guinea pig will not be difficult, but you do need to take the time to learn about his nutritional needs so you can select healthy food for him. In this chapter you will learn the basics about your guinea pig's nutritional needs and receive tips for creating a healthy diet for your new pet. You will also receive tips for the amount to feed your guinea pig, what vegetables he is likely to enjoy, and information about nutritional supplements your guinea pig might require for good health.

1. Nutritional Needs

In the wild, guinea pigs eat a diet of grasses and they are completely herbivorous. In captivity, guinea pigs rely on their owners for food. If you want your Teddy guinea pig to be as healthy as possible you need to familiarize yourself with his nutritional needs so you can create a diet that meets those needs. The foundation of your guinea pig's diet should come from commercially prepared hay pellets. If you walk down the small pet aisle at your local pet store you will see a number of different guinea pig diets. Avoid the bags filled with bright, colorful ingredients and seeds. While these diets may appeal more to your guinea pig, he will likely just pick out the treats and ignore the pellets. Those colorful crunchies are also loaded with artificial ingredients that your guinea pig doesn't need.

Your best bet for guinea pig food is to find a plain pellet. Check the label to make sure that it provides about 18 to 20% protein and 10 to 16% fiber. Guinea pigs do need protein in their diet but too much protein can be harmful. Alfalfa hay is too high in protein for guinea pigs to be used as anything but an occasional treat. Look for timothy hay-based pellets instead.

In addition to protein, fiber is an essential part of the guinea pig's diet. Pellets, fresh hay, and fresh vegetables and fruits are a great source of fiber for your guinea pig. Guinea pigs also need to get Vitamin C from their diets because, like people, they cannot produce it on their own (rabbits can). Guinea pigs also have a higher Vitamin A requirement than other rodents. Their need for calcium, however, is a little lower – too much calcium in the diet can lead to urinary tract problems.

2. Safe Fruits and Vegetables

In addition to feeding your Teddy guinea pig a staple diet of pellets and fresh hay, you should also offer some fresh vegetables and fruits. Do not give your guinea pigs unlimited access to fruits and vegetables but try to give them about ½ cup of vegetables each per day and offer small amounts of fruit once or twice a week. Below you will find a list of fruits and vegetables that are safe for guinea pigs – items that are printed in **bold** are good sources of vitamin C:

Apple	Blackberry	Dandelion
Arugula	Blueberries	greens
Asparagus	Carrots	Dill
Apricot	Cauliflower	Dragon fruit
Avocado	Celieriac	Fennel
Artichoke	Celery	Grass
Banana	Cabbage	Grapefruit
Basil	Chicory	Green beans
Bell peppers	Cilantro	Grapes
Bean sprouts	Corn on the cob	Gooseberries
Beetroot	Cucumber	**Kale**
Broccoli		**Kiwi fruit**

Lemongrass	Papaya	Sweet potato
Lettuce	Pear	Spinach
Mango	Peaches	Squash
Melon	**Parsley**	Swiss chard
Mustard greens	Pumpkin	Tomatoes
Mint	Pineapple	Thyme
Nectarines	Radish	Watercress
Oranges	Raspberries	Zucchini
Parsnips	Sage	
Passion fruit	**Spring greens**	

Before feeding your guinea pig fresh fruits, vegetables, or herbs, make sure that they have not been treated with any chemical pesticides or herbicides. Wash your produce for your guinea pig just as you would wash it for your own consumption. You can feed your guinea pig wild grasses and herbs as long as you are sure that they haven't been sprayed.

3. Feeding Recommendations

As you have already learned, commercial hay pellets should compose the majority of your guinea pig's diet. You can also offer your guinea pig fresh hay and fresh fruits and vegetables. Offer your guinea pig about ¼ to ½ cup of pellets per day plus about ½ cup of fresh vegetables. Fresh fruits should be offered in very small quantities and only once or twice a week as a special treat for your guinea pig.

In addition to food, your guinea pig should have constant access to an unlimited supply of fresh water. Ideally, you should offer your guinea pig chlorine-free water. If your water isn't treated for chlorine, you might want to stick with bottled water or bottled spring water. If you use tap water, consider treating it with a de-chlorinator, the kind you would find in the fish aisle at your local pet store. Avoid using distilled water for your guinea pigs because all of the minerals have been removed and some of those minerals are necessary for your guinea pig's health.

As long as you give your guinea pig fresh fruits and vegetables that are rich in vitamin C once in a while you should not have to worry about nutritional deficiencies. If you are worried that your guinea pig isn't getting enough vitamin C, you can use a liquid nutritional supplement. Vitamin C supplements can be added to your guinea pig's water. Your guinea pig's pellet diet should also contain some Vitamin C – use it while it is fresh because the vitamin content will deteriorate over time.

In addition to pellets and fresh fruits and vegetables you should also offer your guinea pigs an unlimited supply of fresh hay. There are different types of hay that you will find at the pet store and some are better for guinea pigs than others. You will find an overview of the different types of hay below:

Alfalfa Hay – This type of hay is very rich and loaded with protein so it is good for pregnant and nursing guinea pigs as well as pups. Do not give other guinea pigs too much of this hay because it can cause obesity and health problems.

Botanical Hay – This type of hay includes a variety of grasses and dried flowers, which gives your guinea pig many different flavors to enjoy.

Oat Hay – This type of hay is thicker than most hays, which makes it good for grinding your guinea pig's teeth down. Offer some of this hay for variety with your typical hay choice.

Orchard Grass – This type of hay has a soft texture so it is a good choice if you want to use hay as bedding – it also makes a good treat for guinea pigs.

Timothy Hay – This type of hay is the most commonly available and typically favored by guinea pigs.

You can offer your guinea pig hay in a hayrack or a similar device that keeps it off the floor of the cage where it could be contaminated. Keep the hayrack full for happy guinea pigs.

Chapter 6) Training and Handling Your Guinea Pigs

If you have ever kept a dog or cat before, you may already know the basics about training and handling pets. It is important for you to realize, however, that keeping guinea pigs is very different to keeping other, more traditional pets. Not only is their care very different but you also cannot train a guinea pig in the same way that you might train a dog. It is, however, possible to teach your guinea pig to respond to a few simple commands and you may even be able to teach him some tricks. Guinea pigs love food, so using treats is a great way to train them. Some guinea pig owners even have success in "litter training" their guinea pigs. You cannot completely train your guinea pig to be as consistent as a cat in using a litter box but you can take advantage of their tendency to use one area of the cage more than others to go to the bathroom. In this chapter you will learn the basics about training your guinea pig and you will also receive some tips for handling your guinea pig to make sure he stays tame. You will also find information about giving your guinea pig time outside the cage.

1. Teaching Your Guinea Pig Simple Commands

As it has already been mentioned, guinea pigs cannot be trained in the same way that dogs can. However, they are fairly intelligent animals with good memories. If you think back to the beginning of this book you may remember that laboratory guinea pigs have the ability to remember complex routes to food for up to several months. This being the case, you should be able to train your guinea pig to do simple things like come when called and to perform basic tricks.

The key to training your guinea pig lies in rewarding him for performing the behavior you want. Guinea pigs eat almost constantly so they love food – if you give them food as a reward for doing something you want them to do, they will be more likely to repeat that behavior in the future. This is the basic principle behind operant conditioning, or positive-reinforcement training. This is one of the most popular and effective methods for training dogs.

Keep in mind that you will not be able to teach your guinea pig complex tricks all at once. For example, if you wanted to teach your guinea pig to jump through a hoop, you would have to teach him a series of smaller tasks leading up to the main trick.

You might start by getting the guinea pig used to the hoop, then teach him to walk through it, then slowly raise it off the ground a little bit so he has to jump through it. Repetition is very important when training guinea pigs and different tricks will take different lengths of time to teach depending on their complexity and on your guinea pig's intelligence.

Some of the tricks you should be able to teach your guinea pig include the following:

- Come when called by name
- Teaching guinea pig to talk
- Jumping through a hoop
- Picking up items in his mouth
- Turning in a circle
- Standing on his hind legs

Come When Called by Name
This is perhaps the easiest trick to teach and the training process is similar to the one you would use for dogs and cats. Every time you feed your guinea pig, say his name out loud.

You should also say his name every time you pick him up and when transferring him from one person to another. You may also want to give your guinea pig a small treat by hand each time you say his name. With repetition your guinea pig will quickly learn to associate his name with food or fun.

Teaching Guinea Pig to "Talk"

Guinea pigs are fairly vocal as it is, so you may want to think twice before teaching your guinea pig to make noise on command. The best way to train your guinea pig to do this is to take advantage of something that already makes him squeal. For many guinea pigs, the sound of plastic bags rustling is enough to send them into a frenzy because they know food is coming. To use this in training your guinea pig, stand near the cage and say your guinea pig's name to get his attention. Next, give him a verbal command like "talk to me" and immediately rustle the plastic bag. When your guinea pig starts squealing, give him a small food reward. Repeat this sequence a few times until your guinea pig starts to reliably squeal every time you rustle the bag. Then, try doing the trick without rustling the bag, just with the verbal command.

Jumping Through a Hoop

Guinea pigs are not particularly agile, but you can teach them to hop through a hoop as long as you don't hold it very high off the ground. You will need to start by finding a hoop that is about 6- to 10-inches in diameter like a pool diving ring. To begin, hold the hoop in front of your guinea pig when he is in a place that makes him feel safe and comfortable. Say your guinea pig's name while holding a treat on the far side of the hoop. If your guinea pig doesn't move through the hoop to get the treat, give him a little nudge from behind. When he moves through the hoop, give him the treat and use a praise word like "Good". Repeat this sequence over and over until your guinea pig happily walks through the hoop each time. Once your guinea pig consistently moves through the hoop you can start to gradually raise it a little bit off the ground. You should aim for a maximum height of about 1 to 2 inches off the ground.

Picking Up Items in His Mouth

Your guinea pig uses his mouth in the same way that you would use your hand – to pick things up and explore them. You can use this tendency to teach your guinea pig to pick things up on command. The best object to use is a plastic ball cat toy – one with holes or bars in it that your guinea pig can pick up with his teeth. Place your guinea pig on a flat surface like a table and face him towards you with the cat ball in between. Hold a small treat in one hand and use it to lure the guinea pig to the cat ball then give your guinea pig a verbal cue like "take it". When your guinea pig touches the item with any part of his face, give him a bite of the treat – a piece of carrot works well for this trick. Move your guinea pig back to the starting point and repeat the sequence several more times.

Once your guinea pig has started to react consistently you should repeat the sequence and wait for your guinea pig to touch the cat ball. Do not immediately reward him – wait for him to do something letting you know that he is doing what you wanted him to do. Your guinea pig might put his foot on the cat ball or move it with his mouth. If your guinea pig puts his foot on the ball, tell him "no". If he moves the ball with his mouth, praise him and reward him. Once your guinea pig follows your command consistently you can try the training sequence with other items.

Turning in a Circle
This is another fairly easy trick to teach your guinea pig because it utilizes an action the guinea pig does anyway. Place your guinea pig on a flat surface facing towards you and hold a treat in one hand above the guinea pig's head. Give your guinea pig a verbal command like "circle" and move the treat slowly in a circle, leading your guinea pig to follow. After your guinea pig completes the circle, tell him "good" and give him the treat. Repeat the sequence a few times and then try it a day or two later without holding a treat but still using the circular hand motion.

Standing on his hind legs
Guinea pigs do not have the same level of balance as other animals, but you may be able to teach them to stand on their hind legs if you do so through a sequence of training sessions. Place your guinea pig on a flat surface facing towards you and hold a piece of carrot above his head. Give a verbal cue like "stand" or "up". When your guinea pig raises his head to follow the treat and

lifts one foot off the ground, tell him "good" and give him a bite of the treat. Repeat this several times, then end your training session. Later in the day, repeat the sequence but wait for both feet to lift slightly off the ground before praising and rewarding your guinea pig. Repeat this sequence a few times then stop for the day. When you come back to the training later your guinea pig may stand up even higher, resting his rump on the ground. Some guinea pigs will never truly stand on their hind legs so know your guinea pig's limitations and do not push him too hard or he might hurt himself.

2. Litter Training Your Guinea Pig

Guinea pigs tend to do their business wherever it is convenient for them. Many guinea pigs, however, tend to use one particular area of the cage as their bathroom, reserving the rest for playtime and sleep. If your guinea pig does this you will have a higher chance of success in litter training your guinea pig. Keep in mind that you cannot completely litter train a guinea pig but you can encourage him to use one area of the cage as his bathroom in order to make cleanup easier on you.

To litter train your guinea pig, follow the list of steps below:

1. Observe your guinea pigs for a few days and keep an eye on their cage to determine where they like to go to the bathroom. If you have a shelter in the cage, that is the most likely location.

2. Place a litter box designed for rodents in that area – place a handful of hay in the litter box along with a few droppings to make it smell like a bathroom area to your guinea pig.

3. Wait for your guinea pig to come investigate the litter box.

4. If your guinea pig uses the litter box, tell him "good" and offer him a food reward.

5. Repeat this sequence several times a day for several days, rewarding your guinea pig each time he uses the box.

6. Do not punish your guinea pig for going to the bathroom in other parts of the cage, but only reward him when he uses the litter box appropriately.

7. Once your guinea pig is consistently using the litter box, try to see if he will do it outside the cage.

8. Place the litter box outside the cage and wait for your guinea pig to show signs of having to go (such as backing up or fidgeting) – guinea pigs have very small bladders so the usually urinate every 15 minutes or so.

9. When you see your guinea pig getting ready to urinate, pick him up and place him in the litter box.

10. If he does his business there, praise him and reward him with a treat then place him back in the cage.

Again, the key to litter training your guinea pig is to be consistent and to reward him each time he performs the desired behavior. Some guinea pigs learn to use a litter box very quickly while others never really catch on. Repetition is important when training your guinea pig to do anything, including teaching him to use the litter box.

3. Handling Your Guinea Pig

Guinea pigs are naturally nervous animals because they are prey animals, but with proper handling they can get used to people and they may even enjoy being held. Some guinea pigs learn to love being petted and held by their owners so they squeal when their owner comes into the room or stand on their hind legs, begging to be picked up. The most important thing to remember when handling your guinea pig is that it is fragile – guinea pigs have very small bones and rough handling could hurt them quite easily, especially if you drop them.

In order to properly handle your guinea pig you need to learn how to safely pick him up from the cage. Try to approach your guinea pig from the front, not from the rear, so he sees you coming and is less frightened. Speak gently to your guinea pig, using his name, when you get close to him and try to stroke him gently along his back to calm him down. After a few strokes, gently slide one hand under the guinea pig's chest (right behind the front feet) and slide the other hand under his rump. Maintain a firm grip on your guinea pig to keep him from jumping out of your hands, but do not squeeze him. Lift the guinea pig out of the cage and bring him in to your chest. Hold the guinea pig against your body with one hand under his rump and the other on his back, keeping him close to your body.

While your guinea pig is getting used to being handled it is a good idea to hold him while kneeling or sitting down – this means that if your guinea pig struggles and breaks loose that he will not have a far way to fall. If your guinea pig starts to squirm, you can hold him a little tighter and try stroking him until he calms down. If he appears to be very frightened, however, you should put him back in the cage before he jumps out of your hands and possibly hurts himself.

If you have children in your household you need to teach them how to properly handle the guinea pig for their safety and for the guinea pig's. Teach your children to kneel by the cage or to sit on the floor while you pick up the guinea pig and bring it to them. Instruct your children to hold the guinea pig firmly but gently against their chest – show them how to support the rump with one hand and to use the other hand to support the guinea pig's back. Do not let your children walk around while carrying the guinea pig – make sure they stay seated. If your child is under the age of four, never let them take the guinea pig out of the cage themselves. Older children can be taught the right way to lift a guinea pig from the cage.

Guinea pigs can become quite tame with regular handling and some will learn to love being petted. You shouldn't carry your guinea pig around the house with you all day, however, because you will end up with very soiled clothes. You should only hold your guinea pig for about 10 minutes at a time because guinea pigs go to the bathroom very frequently. Sometimes your guinea pig will let you know that he needs to be put down by squirming or whining. To help protect your clothes you can place a towel under the guinea pig.

While most guinea pigs learn to like being handled, this may not be the case with pregnant guinea pigs. You need to be very careful and gentle with pregnant guinea pigs because not only do you risk harming her, but you could also hurt the babies developing inside her. It is okay to handle a pregnant guinea pig in the early stages of pregnancy, but do not handle her once she starts to become visibly larger. It is especially important that you do not poke and prod her, trying to feel the babies. If you have to take her to the vet, place a small cat carrier in the cage with a trail of veggies leading into it so she will go inside on her own.

4. Letting Your Guinea Pig Out of the Cage

Because your guinea pig spends most of his life inside his cage, it is a good idea to let him have some playtime out of the cage whenever possible. You should not let your guinea pig run loose in the house at all times because he could crawl into a tight space and get stuck – this might also put him at risk of harm by other household pets like dogs or cats. If you want to give your guinea pig some play time outside the cage you should build him a playpen that you can move around the house.

If you built your own C&C cage to house your guinea pigs you can use a few extra grids to create a playpen. Simply attach the grids to each other in a square or rectangular shape and place it in an open area where your guinea pig can run freely inside the pen. Ideally, you should place the pen on top of an old towel or a few pieces of newspaper to soak up any urine and to prevent stains. If you have an old piece of carpet, you can use that as well. You can even take your guinea pig's playpen outside as long as the weather is nice. If you do, make sure you use extra grids to cover the top of the playpen or cover it with a blanket or a piece of cardboard. This will help to keep your guinea pigs protected from wild animals and it will give them some shade on a sunny day.

You can choose whether to give your guinea pigs out-of-the-cage playtime individually or together. Sometimes guinea pigs that are kept in groups appreciate having a little time to themselves, especially if one of the other guinea pigs in the cage is antagonistic. When your guinea pig is running around in a playpen is when you are most likely to see the behavior called "popcorning". Guinea pigs love to explore new places so add some cardboard boxes, tunnels, stuffed animals, and other objects to the playpen for your guinea pig to explore. Just make sure not to stuff it too full that your guinea pig can't run around.

5. Introducing New Guinea Pigs

As you have already learned, guinea pigs are very social animals and they should be kept in pairs or small groups. Ideally, you should keep guinea pigs that were born in the same litter so that they are already used to each other – this will reduce the likelihood of problems between your guinea pigs. If you buy your guinea pigs separately, however, they can still get along – you just have to be careful about how you introduce them to each other to make sure they bond.

Guinea pigs that are kept in a group together will form a natural pecking order, or hierarchy, and you need to let it happen even if it means that your guinea pigs might fight for a while. If you want to add a new guinea pig to the group, introduce them in a space that is completely neutral – do not just add the new guinea pig to the cage. Give the guinea pigs time to get used to each other and do not be surprised if you see some aggressive behavior. Male guinea pigs will chatter their teeth at each other and they may chase each other around the cage. To avoid problems with aggression, try housing one neutered male with one or more females rather than keeping several intact males together. No matter what type of grouping you choose, make sure you provide plenty of hiding spaces where the guinea pigs can get away if they need to.

Chapter 7) Breeding Teddy Guinea Pigs

If you are thinking about breeding your Teddy guinea pig to make some extra money, think again – profit should never be the primary motivation for breeding an animal. Breeding can be very stressful on your guinea pig, especially for females, and there is a fairly high risk of complications during birth. If your intention in breeding your Teddy guinea pig is to improve the breed or to produce show-quality Teddy guinea pigs, that is a different story. In either case, it is essential that you learn everything you can about breeding guinea pigs before you give it a try – this is the best way to ensure that your guinea pigs stay healthy and safe during breeding. In this chapter you will find an overview of basic guinea pig breeding information as well as tips for initiating the breeding process, caring for pregnant guinea pig sows, and raising the pups after birth.

1. Basic Breeding Info

Before you decide to breed your Teddy guinea pig you need to learn the basics about guinea pig breeding. Only once you have a thorough understanding of the breeding process for guinea pigs can you really know if you are up to the challenge. In this section you will find detailed information about guinea pig breeding to help you make your decision.

Guinea pigs reach sexual maturity at the age of ten weeks, though it technically can happen as early as four weeks. For this reason, guinea pig litters are usually divided by sex before they reach four weeks of age. Though guinea pigs are physically capable of breeding at this age, you should not breed a guinea pig that young. Ideally, you should never breed a female guinea pig (sow) before 4 months of age or a weight of 500 to 600 grams (1.1 to 1.3 lbs.).

71

Not only is there a minimum age to start breeding female guinea pigs, but there is a maximum age as well. If your female guinea pig does not produce a litter before she reaches 12 months of age it can be very dangerous to breed her after that point. If you do not breed your female before 12 months of age, the ligaments around the pelvic bone may become rigid, which will make it nearly impossible for her to have a natural birth – you will need to perform a C-section to remove the babies and this can be extremely dangerous for guinea pigs. Not every female guinea pig over the age of 12 months will have this problem but it is definitely not a risk you want to take.

Female guinea pigs become fertile again immediately after giving birth, so it is important to keep them separated from male guinea pigs to avoid having litters too close together. The female will need time to rest before becoming pregnant again – you should wait at least 3 or 4 months between breeding sessions. This will give you a maximum of two litters per year to ensure the safety of your female guinea pig. You should also think about retiring your female after 2 years or so to avoid putting too much strain on her body. She will have produced two or three litters by then, which is more than enough for one guinea pig.

Breeding can be very dangerous and taxing for female guinea pigs and it is completely possible (and not uncommon) for a healthy litter of pups to be born just for the mother to die a day or two later. Pregnancy and delivery complications are fairly common with female guinea pigs often succumbing to infection, toxemia, or blood loss. If you are breeding multiple guinea pigs at the same time you may be able to get another female to foster the litter. If not, you might have to hand-feed the babies using a small mammal milk formula called Divetalact. Even if you are able to get the babies to accept the formula they may still die after a few days simply because nothing compares to a mother's milk.

2. The Breeding Process

In order to breed your Teddy guinea pigs, you will need to learn how to tell the two sexes apart. It is possible to sex a guinea pig at birth if you know what to look for but most people find it easier to wait until the guinea pig has grown up a little. To sex your guinea pig, hold him gently with his belly up, supporting his back with your hand. Locate the anus then look directly above it – a male will have a small slit just above the anus and, in adults, you will be able to clearly see the testes. For females you may notice a Y-shaped fold of skin above the anus in addition to an external urethral opening.

Female guinea pigs experience an estrus cycle that lasts about 14 to 19 days. The estrus cycle is simply the period of time during which the female is most fertile and receptive to mating. Some female guinea pigs can reach sexual maturity as early as 2 months and, once they do, they may come in and out of heat about every two or three weeks. During the female's estrus cycle there is about a ½-day period of time during which she will be receptive to breeding. You will notice this happening because she might start mounting other guinea pigs in the cage, even if they are female. If you intend to breed your guinea pigs, this is when you should introduce the female to the male.

If you introduce the female guinea pig to the male and they are both receptive to breeding, it should not take long for the process to occur. If the female is receptive, she may arch her back and lift her hindquarters as the male approaches. If she is not, she might spray him with urine, lunge at him, or rear up and swat his face while showing her teeth. When the breeding process is successfully completed and the female becomes pregnant she will enter a gestation period lasting between 65 and 70 days. The average litter size for guinea pigs is between 2 and 4 pups but it is possible to have a litter of 7 or more.

As the pups develop in the female's womb, she will noticeably increase in size. Her abdomen will become distended and she will double or triple her food and water intake. The best way to tell whether a female is pregnant is to weigh her on a daily basis – if she shows a steady increase in weight it is a good bet that she is pregnant. Eventually she will start to take on a pear shape that will be another good indication of pregnancy. During pregnancy you should avoid making any changes to your female guinea pig's cage because it could stress her out and she might stop eating and drinking.

3. Raising the Babies

Guinea pigs typically do not make any preparations for birth so you do not need to worry about providing a nesting box. One thing you need to be careful about is the fact that pheromones released from a female guinea pig in labor can trigger premature labor in other pregnant guinea pigs if they are housed in close proximity. For this reason it is important that you move your pregnant females into another room when they are nearing the expected delivery date. If you have two females that became pregnant at the same time you can keep them together – they may even help to clean and raise each other's pups.

When a female guinea pig nears her due date, the area between her pelvic bones will begin to dilate. This dilation usually begins about 1 to 2 weeks before the birth and it opens to the maximum amount (about 2 fingers' width) about 24 hours before birth. For female guinea pigs, labor typically lasts about 10 to 30 minutes with a space of 5 to 10 minutes between each birth. Guinea pigs give birth by sitting up and hunching their bodies or squatting then straining to expel the fetus. The sow will clean each pup and consume the placenta as well.

When guinea pig pups are born, they already have some hair, a full set of teeth, and their eyes are already opened. Additionally, baby guinea pigs are ready to run from the moment they are born. Guinea pig pups will rely on their mother for food and warmth for 14 to 21 days, though the sow may not pay much attention to them. Male guinea pigs typically do not take part in raising the babies and the female might actually ignore the pups for the most part. It is rare, however, for guinea pigs to eat their young.

It is necessary to separate female pups from their father before 21 days of age to prevent unwanted breeding – you may also want to separate the male and female pups in the same litter at this time. This is also the time that guinea pig pups will usually wean themselves off their mother's milk. Once they have been weaned you can treat the pups like adults. You should start handling the pups as soon as the parents will tolerate it to make sure that they are tamed and grow up to be friendly with people.

Chapter 8) Keeping Your Guinea Pig Healthy

The best thing you can do in order to keep your Teddy guinea pig healthy is to provide him with a clean habitat and a healthy diet. Even if you provide these things, however, your guinea pig may still be susceptible to certain diseases. You may not be able to completely prevent your guinea pig from ever getting sick, but you can take steps to ensure that if he does you will be prepared. In order to ensure a fast and successful recovery for your guinea pig you should take the time to learn the basics about common diseases affecting these animals as well as their causes, symptoms, and treatment options. In this chapter you will find an overview of common guinea pig diseases so you will be able to identify them if your Teddy guinea pig ever gets sick. You will also find some general information for preventing disease in your guinea pig in this chapter.

1. Common Health Problems

If your guinea pig becomes sick, your ability to diagnose the disease and start treatment will affect his likelihood of making a full recovery. In order to make sure that you get your guinea pig the treatment he needs as quickly as possible you should take the time to familiarize yourself with common guinea pig diseases. In this section you'll find an overview of common diseases affecting guinea pigs as well as information about their cause, symptoms, and treatment options.

Some of the most common diseases known to affect guinea pigs include the following:

- Barbering
- Bumble Foot
- Calcium Deficiency
- Conjunctivitis

- Diarrhea
- Ear Infections
- Fur Mites
- Ketosis
- Malocclusion
- Mastitis
- Metastatic Calcification
- Pneumonia
- Ringworm
- Scurvy
- Swollen Lymph Nodes
- Urinary Problems

Barbering
Guinea pigs may experience a variety of different types of hair loss. In some cases it is related to a fungal infection (like ringworm) but in other cases it is not. One of the most common causes for hair loss in guinea pigs is a condition called barbering in which the guinea pig actually chews or tears its own hair out. Hair loss may also occur when a male guinea pig is fighting another male for dominance and the other male chews or tears out the opponent's fur. Barbering can also occur in female guinea pigs that are very stressed.

You can tell that a guinea pig is barbering simply by looking at the hair – it will appear to be very short and chewed off near the skin, leaving a bald patch. The skin under the chewed hair may also be bruised or inflamed. In some cases, the skin may actually be broken and this puts the guinea pig at risk of infection. Keep a close eye on areas of barbering to make sure that they do not become infected.

Diagnosis of barbering is usually easy to make by a simple visual examination. Because there are several potential causes for this condition, however, it is a good idea to rule out possibilities one by one. Provide your veterinarian with as much information as you can about your guinea pig's behavior and condition to help him make the correct diagnosis. If you can, keep track of the onset of symptoms and the progression of the hair loss as well as any potential contributing factors like fighting with other guinea pigs in the cage.

Aside from barbering by other guinea pigs and self-barbering, hair loss in guinea pigs can also sometimes be a genetic problem – it might also be due to metabolic problems or dietary deficiencies. In some cases, hair loss is just a natural consequence of aging. In very young guinea pigs, the coat might thin a little bit during the weaning process and then grow back into a thicker, coarser adult coat after the transition has been made. You will not need to treat this type of hair loss, just make sure your guinea pig gets enough protein in its diet.

Treatments for hair loss in guinea pigs vary depending on the cause. If the hair loss is due to a metabolic condition it might be treated with medications or lifestyle changes. Hair loss due to dietary deficiencies can be treated with supplements or a special diet. Unfortunately, hair loss caused by genetic factors cannot be controlled or treated. If it is due to barbering, however, there are a few things you can try. Separating the guinea pigs that are fighting or increasing the cage size can help to reduce stress levels as well as barbering behavior. Feeding your guinea pig a healthy diet will help him to re grow his coat and to regain healthy coat condition.

Bumble Foot
Also known as pododermatitis, bumble foot is a condition that commonly affects the footpad in guinea pigs. This condition is a bacterial infection, in most cases, which causes the guinea pig's footpad to become inflamed, to become overgrown, or to develop sores. The sores may look similar to calluses in appearance but the accompanying swelling and inflammation is a good indication of infection. If bumble foot in guinea pigs goes untreated it can progress to a very dangerous state – the guinea pig may develop secondary complications or the entire leg might become infected, necessitating an amputation.

The symptoms of bumble foot are generally easy to recognize by visual exam. The footpad will become red and inflamed and it might develop sores over the course of a few months. You might also notice hair loss on the affected foot and swelling in the joints or tendons of the affected leg. As the infection progresses your guinea pig might be reluctant to move or unable to move normally – he may also experience a loss of appetite in response to the pain. In some cases, guinea pigs experience protein deposits (amyloid deposition) in the liver, kidneys, hormone glands, and the pancreas.

The primary cause of bumble foot is the *Staphylococcus aureus* bacteria, which can enter the guinea pig's footpad through tiny cuts or scrapes. There are also a number of underlying factors that contribute to bumble foot. These factors may include obesity or excessive pressure on the feet, overgrown nails, nutritional deficiencies (especially Vitamin C), wire floor in the cage, injury to the foot, poor sanitation, or excessive humidity.

In order to make a diagnosis of your guinea pig's condition your veterinarian will need to take a thorough history of his diet, health, living conditions, and the onset of symptoms. Blood or fluid samples may also be taken to confirm a diagnosis of bumble foot, or pododermatitis. If the *Staphylococcus aureus* bacteria are to blame, the exact train will need to be identified in order for an effective treatment to be prescribed. In severe cases, your vet might prescribe antibiotic medications and/or pain medication in addition to environmental and lifestyle changes.

As long as you detect bumble foot early, making changes to your guinea pig's cage may be enough to get the infection under control. Improving sanitation and switching to a softer bedding might help – if you are using a wire-bottom cage, you will need to switch that out as well. Keep the cage floor dry and clean – a damp floor will provide a breeding ground for bacteria and it will soften the tissue on the bottom of your guinea pig's feet, making it more susceptible to infection. Increasing your guinea pig's daily dose of Vitamin C may also help to stave off infection.

If your guinea pig's pododermatitis has already begun to progress, your veterinarian may clean the wound and clip the hair around the affected area. Overgrown nails and dead tissue might also need to be trimmed away. In some cases, soaking the foot in an antibiotic or saltwater solution might help. No matter which treatment option you go with, make sure to clean and disinfect your guinea pig's cage before placing him back inside it. Take precautions to keep the cage clean and dry during treatment and, if necessary, keep the foot bandaged. Follow your veterinarian's instructions closely for treatment and bandaging.

Calcium Deficiency
Providing your guinea pig with a healthy diet is the number one way to keep him in good health. Guinea pigs, like all animals, are prone to nutritional deficiencies so they require a balance of various nutrients in their diets. One of the most important nutrients for guinea pigs is calcium. Calcium is required for healthy skeletal growth and development, especially in young guinea pigs, and it helps with milk production in pregnant and nursing females. In pregnant females, calcium deficiency usually occurs about one to two weeks before giving birth or shortly after. Guinea pigs that are obese or highly stressed, as well as sows that have had multiple pregnancies, are also at a higher risk of developing a calcium deficiency.

The symptoms associated with calcium deficiency are very similar to the signs of pregnancy toxemia. Pregnancy toxemia is blood poisoning – it occurs when toxic substances (often bacteria) are present in the blood. The difference between pregnancy toxemia and calcium deficiency is that the symptoms of the former are more severe and more likely to become fatal. Some of the symptoms associated with calcium deficiency include depression, dehydration, muscle spasms, loss of appetite, and convulsions. Some guinea pigs may actually die from this condition without ever showing symptoms.

In pregnant guinea pigs, calcium deficiency is related to an increased requirement for calcium to support fetal growth, nursing, and the birthing process. This condition can also affect obese guinea pigs, stressed guinea pigs, and sows that have been pregnant multiple times. In order to diagnose calcium deficiency, your veterinarian will need to take a medical history, diet history, and he will ask about incidents that could have contributed to the development of the disease. A differential diagnosis may be required, especially since the symptoms are so close to those of pregnancy toxemia. A blood test for calcium levels may be taken to confirm a diagnosis of calcium deficiency.

The treatment for calcium deficiency in guinea pigs is the administration of dietary supplements. Your veterinarian will be able to tell you what kind of dosage to follow and will prescribe a certain type of supplement. In addition to dietary supplements you should also make sure that your guinea pig's diet is nutritious and well balanced. Feed your guinea pig a high-quality commercial pellet diet supplemented with fresh hay and fresh vegetables. Some vegetables that are high in calcium include kale, collard greens, broccoli, spinach, turnip greens, and arugula.

Conjunctivitis
Conjunctivitis in guinea pigs is known by several different nicknames including "pink eye" and "red eye". While this condition on its own is not particularly dangerous, the underlying cause of the infection may lead to secondary infections and other complications. Conjunctivitis is simply the inflammation of the outermost layer of the eye. There are two types of bacteria that are common causes for this condition – *Streptococcus* and *Bordetella*. Before treating your guinea pig with any antibiotic medications you need to consult your veterinarian. Guinea pigs are very sensitive to antibiotics so they have a high risk of developing allergic reactions. Treating a guinea pig with certain antibiotics like penicillins could be fatal.
The common symptoms of conjunctivitis in guinea pigs include pus-filled discharge, watery eyes, swelling or inflammation of the tissues around the eye, redness of the eyelids, and sticky eyelids

from dried discharge. As you have already learned, bacteria like *Streptococcus* and *Bordetella* are the most common causes for this condition, though upper respiratory tract infections could be a contributing factor as well. In order to make a diagnosis of conjunctivitis, your veterinarian will examine the discharge or pus coming from the eye to identify the type of bacteria (or other infectious agent) causing the problem.

Treatment options for conjunctivitis may vary from one case to another depending on the bacteria responsible for the infection. In most cases, treatment involves antibiotic eye drops, sometimes paired with an oral antibiotic to help control the primary infection. The best way to administer eye drops for a guinea pig is to wrap him gently in a towel and to lay him on his back. You may need to use one hand to gently hold the eye open as you administer the eye drops. Wrapping the guinea pig in a towel will keep him from scratching you if he starts to scramble.

Before you take your guinea pig home, your veterinarian will probably clean and remove any discharge from the eye using antiseptic eyewash. You may be given some of this eye wash to take and use at home – if you are, make sure you have the vet show you how to use it properly. As your guinea pig recovers from conjunctivitis you need to keep his cage clean and do everything you can to keep his stress levels low. Clean the infected eye regularly using the antiseptic eye wash and administer the eye drops as directed. Monitor your guinea pig's reaction to the medications closely and report any changes in behavior or condition immediately to your vet.

Diarrhea
Guinea pig droppings typically consist of firm, dry pellets of an oblong shape. If you notice a change in your guinea pig's stool, it is a good bet that something is wrong. In some cases, it could be a result of something he ate, but most of the time it is an indication of infection or some kind of disease. Diarrhea in guinea pigs is the result of digestive upset, which can be caused by dietary changes, disease, or infection. Treatment for diarrhea is very

important because if you leave it your guinea pig could become dehydrated and that could lead to death.

Guinea pigs affected by diarrhea may exhibit additional symptoms including lethargy, dehydration, loss of appetite, dull or depressed appearance, and rough coat condition. You may also notice your guinea pig exhibiting a hunched posture and his eyes may appear to be sunken in. Guinea pigs suffering from diarrhea may have soiling in the fur near the anus and they might also have an abnormally low body temperature. The symptoms that accompany diarrhea may vary according to the cause of the problem, which could be related to various viral, bacterial, or parasitic infections. A diet that is too low in fiber can also lead to diarrhea in guinea pigs.

Your veterinarian will make a diagnosis based primarily on the observation of clinical signs. The diagnosis will then be confirmed with a dietary and medical history – your vet might also take blood or stool samples to identify the infectious agent causing the problem. Treatment options for diarrhea may vary according to the primary cause, though giving your guinea pig plenty of water will be very important in all cases. If your guinea pig refuses to drink your veterinarian may administer IV fluids to help rehydrate him. In some cases, antibiotics may be necessary to treat the infection, though guinea pigs sometimes don't react well to antibiotics and they may worsen the imbalance of beneficial bacteria in your guinea pig's digestive tract.

In addition to rehydrating your guinea pig, you will also need to make some changes to his diet to prevent the diarrhea from recurring. Make sure your guinea pig's diet is rich in fiber by providing plenty of roughage like fresh hay. It may also be beneficial for you to feed your guinea pig small amounts of yogurt that contains active cultures or use a commercial probiotic supplement. This will help to restore the natural balance of bacteria in your guinea pig's digestive tract. In the case of certain infections you may also need to clean and disinfect your guinea pig's cage and cage accessories.

Ear Infections

Ear infections in guinea pigs are much less common than they are in dogs and cats, but they can still happen. In most cases, guinea pig ear infections are the result of a bacterial infection or some type of respiratory disease. Ear infections usually begin in the outer regions of the ear but they can spread to the middle or inner ear, at which point they become very serious and dangerous for your guinea pig. If you suspect that your guinea pig has an ear infection, you should contact your veterinarian immediately.

Some of the most common signs of ear infections in guinea pigs include discharge or pus in the ears, ear pain, loss of hearing, or total deafness. If the infection spreads to the middle ear or inner ear your guinea pig might also display some behavioral changes like loss of balance, head tilting, walking in circles, or rolling on the ground. The two most common causes of ear infections in guinea pigs are bacterial infections and respiratory diseases like pneumonia and upper respiratory tract infection.

In order to diagnose an ear infection, your veterinarian will observe your guinea pig's clinical signs – he may also ask you about behavioral changes you've noticed to determine whether the infection has spread to the middle or inner ear. In some cases, your vet might test the discharge or pus from the ear to identify the particular infectious agent that is causing the infection. Treatment options will vary depending on the cause of the infection.

First, your vet will probably prescribe medications or a local anesthetic agent to address the symptoms of the ear infection and to reduce your guinea pig's pain. Antibiotic eardrops may also be used to control discharge and to provide temporary pain relief. Antibiotic or antiseptic ear washes may also help to reduce discharge buildup. Treatments aimed at the infection itself are usually not effective, that is why your vet will likely treat the symptoms instead. As your guinea pig recovers from the infection you should keep his cage as clean as possible and reduce his stress levels as well. Take your guinea pig in for a follow-up appointment as directed by your vet and keep using any prescription medications or eardrops.

Fur Mites

One of the most common skin problems known to affect guinea pigs is fur mite infestation. Even when you keep your guinea pig's cage clean and he is healthy, he will still probably carry a few fur mites. The mites will be small and they will not have a negative impact on your guinea pig's health. When your guinea pig becomes stressed or when sanitation in your guinea pig's cage decreases, the mites will multiply and start to become a problem. Mite infestations can also occur secondary to illness or injury and when your guinea pig's ability to groom normally becomes compromised.

The symptoms of fur mites are usually not difficult to identify, though some of them do overlap with other conditions. The most common sign of fur mites is excessive itching and inflammation of the skin. Fur mites can actually burrow into your guinea pig's skin, which not only causes the inflammation and itching but can cause hair loss as well. The types of fur mites that burrow into the skin are usually found on the shoulders, thighs, and neck of the infested guinea pig. Infestations of this type of mite usually produce dry, crusty skin at the burrowing site – the fur may also be oily and the skin thickened.

In cases of severe infestations the areas affected by mites may become infected. This secondary infection may lead to weight loss, low energy, or agitation in the affected guinea pig. If the infestation is allowed to progress without treatment your guinea pig could eventually suffer from convulsions and might even die. The primary causes of fur mite infestation include infection from contaminated objects (like bedding), infection from other guinea pigs, unsanitary living conditions, high stress levels, and lowered immune system due to injury or illness.

Your veterinarian will most likely diagnose a fur mite infestation by performing a physical exam. He will look at your guinea pig's skin for signs of an infestation and may take skin scrapings to check for mites. Treatment options will vary depending on the type of mite and the severity of the infestation. In most cases, your veterinarian will prescribe a powder or spray that can be applied to your guinea pig's skin. Your guinea pig may also require a series of injections to treat the irritation and inflammation caused by the mites.

The key to treating fur mite infestations in guinea pigs is to improve the sanitary conditions in your guinea pig's cage. Fur mites are opportunistic creatures – they are always present on your guinea pig in small numbers but when his system becomes weakened by stress, illness, or unsanitary conditions, the mites will take advantage of it and multiply like crazy. Follow your veterinarian's treatment plan closely and keep your guinea pig's cage as clean as possible. Disinfect the cage after you start treatment to kill any mites and eggs that are already present so they do not cause a re-infestation. You should also keep a close eye on your guinea pig to make sure he is improving with treatment.

Ketosis
Another name for ketosis in guinea pigs is pregnancy toxemia. Ketone bodies are a type of water-soluble compound found in the body – they are the byproduct of breaking down fatty acids, which is a normal metabolic process. In normal conditions, a guinea pig's body is able to excrete ketone bodies at a rate that complements their production. In some cases, however, the production of ketone bodies exceeds the guinea pig's ability to excrete them – this leads to an excess of ketone bodies in the blood, a state referred to as pregnancy toxemia or ketosis. This condition is most commonly seen in pregnant sows during the last two to three weeks of pregnancy or within the first week after giving birth to a litter.

Under normal circumstances, ketone bodies are utilized as an energy source in your guinea pig's body when blood sugar levels drop too low. Your guinea pig's blood sugar levels might drop

86

when no food is available or if his diet is too low in sugar. Ketosis most commonly affects female guinea pigs that are pregnant with their first or second litters and though it is most common in females, it can also occur in obese guinea pigs of either sex.

A guinea pig can develop ketosis without displaying any outward signs; it may even die without every showing symptoms. Ketosis can also cause death of the fetuses inside a pregnant guinea pig. Some of the signs guinea pigs with ketosis may exhibit include loss of appetite, lack of energy, decreased water consumption, muscle spasms, loss of coordination, and coma. The primary cause of ketosis is an excess of ketone bodies in the blood but this could be the result of several underlying factors, which may include loss of appetite during pregnancy, lack of exercise during pregnancy, obesity, large litter sizes, stress levels, and underdeveloped blood vessels in the uterus resulting from a hereditary condition.

In order to diagnose your guinea pig with ketosis, your veterinarian will perform an in-depth examination as well as a dietary and medical history. Your vet will need to make a differential diagnosis to rule out calcium deficiency, another condition that commonly affects pregnant guinea pigs. Blood tests and urinalysis will help to confirm the diagnosis by showing increased ketone bodies in the blood.

Unfortunately, once your guinea pig starts to show signs of ketosis there is a low chance of recovery. Treatment for this condition usually doesn't help but there are some options available including medications like propylene glycol, steroids, or calcium glutamate. If your guinea pig does recover you will need to make sure she has time to recover in a clean, stress-free environment. Ask your veterinarian about any dietary changes you should make and take steps to avoid obesity. Feeding your pregnant guinea pig a high-quality diet will help to prevent her from developing ketosis, or pregnancy toxemia.

Malocclusion
There are several dental diseases known to affect guinea pigs, but the most common is malocclusion. Malocclusion is just another word for improper alignment of teeth. When your guinea pig's teeth become overgrown they might also become misaligned, which could lead to a condition known as slobbers – this is when your guinea pig has difficulty swallowing or chewing as a result of misaligned teeth, which causes him to salivate excessively. Both of these dental conditions require immediate veterinary care for your guinea pig.

The main symptoms of malocclusion in guinea pigs are improper alignment of the teeth, bleeding from the mouth, oral abscesses, sinus infection, weight loss, and difficulty eating. When your guinea pig eats you may see pieces of food coming out the sides of his mouth. As your guinea pig grows, so do his teeth. In fact, his teeth will keep growing throughout his life. Unless you give your guinea pig chew toys and roughage to help wear down his teeth, they could become overgrown and misaligned. Some other causes for malocclusion may include heredity, dietary imbalance, or injury.

In order to make a diagnosis of malocclusion for your guinea pig, your veterinarian will perform a physical exam. He will not only check the length of your guinea pig's teeth but their alignment as well – he will also check for signs of abscesses or other abnormalities in your guinea pig's mouth. Treatment options for malocclusion may vary depending on the cause of the problem. If your guinea pig is drooling excessively it is likely a problem with the molars at the back of the mouth, not the front teeth. Your veterinarian might clip the guinea pig's teeth and may also prescribe calcium or vitamin C supplements.

Mastitis
Mastitis is a condition that affects female guinea pigs and it is characterized by inflammation of the mammary glands, or milk glands. This inflammation is most commonly caused by bacterial infections and it usually occurs after a litter has been born and the

pups are suckling. Another leading cause of mastitis in guinea pigs is cuts or scrapes to the mammary tissue, which presents an opportunity for bacterial infections. Mastitis is very painful for your guinea pig and, without treatment, it can become very serious – the infection could spread to the bloodstream and lead to even more severe complications.

When a guinea pig suffers from mastitis you will notice that the mammary tissues become swollen, tender, warm to the touch, enlarged, painful, and they may be bluish in color. In some cases they will excrete thick, clotted, or bloody milk. If the condition goes untreated it may lead to a systemic infection and the following symptoms – fever, dehydration, loss of appetite, depression, and depleted milk supply. Bacteria can enter the mammary tissue through abrasions to the tissue or through the ducts themselves. A nursing sow it at a higher risk for this condition when she is dehydrated, sick, stressed, or improperly nourished through diet.

Newborn guinea pig pups already have teeth when they are born so they can accidentally injure the mammary tissue during suckling. Even a small abrasion can become an entry point for dangerous bacteria, which can lead to infection of the mammary tissue, or mastitis. To prevent this condition you should perform routine checks of your nursing sow to make sure there are no abrasions in the tissue. If you find any abrasions, or if your guinea pig starts to display symptoms, you should seek veterinary care immediately before the infection spreads to the bloodstream. If your sow develops a systemic infection it could also cause the milk to dry up and your pups could starve.

Your veterinarian will make a diagnosis of mastitis primarily based on symptom observation, though a medical history will be helpful as well. Your vet might take a sample of milk or fluid from the mammary glands to confirm a diagnosis of mastitis – blood tests may also be required to identify the infectious agent causing the problem. Treatment options may vary depending on the type of infection, though antibiotics are common for this type of condition. Your vet may also prescribe antihistamines or anti-inflammatory medications to reduce inflammation. If the mammary tissue has been damaged, your vet will clean and dress the wound.

While your sow is recovering from mastitis it is a good idea to keep the pups away from her so they do not aggravate the condition. If you have another nursing sow you can transfer them to her. If not, you may need to hand-feed the pups for a few days. Make sure to administer any antibiotic medications for the full course recommended by your veterinarian and follow his instructions to keep the wound clean and dressed properly. Maintaining proper sanitation in the cage environment will help to prevent mastitis – you should also stick with soft bedding that will not irritate the skin. Try to keep your guinea pig's stress levels low as well – a stressed guinea pig is more susceptible to disease than a healthy guinea pig.

Metastatic Calcification
Metastatic calcification occurs when calcium deposits harden in the internal organs. This condition can spread throughout your guinea pig's body without producing symptoms, which makes it very dangerous. Many guinea pigs affected by this condition die suddenly without ever showing outward signs of being sick. This condition is most likely to affect male guinea pigs over 1 year of age and the symptoms may include weight loss, muscle/joint stiffness, joint pain, dull or depressed appearance, and increased urination caused by kidney failure. The main cause of metastatic calcification in guinea pigs is a diet that is too high in calcium and phosphorus but low in magnesium.

In order to make a diagnosis of metastatic calcification in your guinea pig, your veterinarian will need to take a history of his health and diet. Observation of clinical signs will also be helpful in making a diagnosis but, again, many guinea pigs do not show outward signs. In some cases the only way to confirm a diagnosis is to take an x-ray of the organs along with blood and fluid samples taken for lab analysis.

Unfortunately, metastatic calcification is difficult to treat once it has gotten to the point that your vet can make an accurate diagnosis. When the condition is diagnosed in the late stages it may only be possible to treat the symptoms, not the actual disease. In some severe cases where the condition cannot be reversed or treated, euthanasia may be the kindest option. If your guinea pig is diagnosed early, there are a few things that your veterinarian might try. Keeping your guinea pig separated from others will help to make sure he gets the rest he needs to recover. Making healthy changes to your guinea pig's diet to ensure balanced nutrition will also be important.

The best way to treat metastatic calcification is to catch it before it becomes a problem. Feeding your guinea pig a high-quality commercial pellet diet is the best way to prevent nutritional diseases like this. Most high-quality commercial guinea pig pellet diets are formulated with an adequate balance of calcium and phosphorus with adequate levels of magnesium to ensure that metastatic calcification doesn't become a problem. Always check the nutrition label for commercial foods before offering them to your guinea pig and do not give him any nutritional supplements unless directed by your veterinarian.

Pneumonia
Some of the most common diseases seen in guinea pigs are respiratory infections like pneumonia. Pneumonia is caused by the *Streptococci pneumonie* bacteria and your guinea pig might not show any outward signs of infection. In many cases, guinea pigs with pneumonia appear to be fine for a time and then they suddenly develop symptoms. Guinea pigs with pneumonia often display signs of stress and they often stop eating, which contributes to death. It is also important to realize that pneumonia is highly infectious – one guinea pig can infect another through direct contact or through coughing and sneezing.

Though many guinea pigs will not show signs of pneumonia in the early stages, some of the symptoms of this disease that you may notice could include sneezing, a dull or depressed appearance, loss of appetite, weight loss, and fever or elevated body temperature. Some internal symptoms that you might not notice include inflammation of the ear, inflammation of the lungs or heart, enlarged lymph nodes, joint inflammation (arthritis), and respiratory distress.

When it comes to making a diagnosis of pneumonia, your veterinarian will observe your guinea pig's clinical symptoms. He may also take a thorough medical history. Certain blood tests, urine tests, and tests of the mucus discharge from the lungs will be used to confirm a diagnosis of pneumonia by checking for the *Streptococci pneumonie* bacteria. In terms of treatment, antibiotics are the most common treatment for pneumonia. Unfortunately, antibiotics can be very dangerous for small animals like guinea pigs so your veterinarian may choose to offer supportive therapy instead with fluid treatment and vitamin/mineral supplements.

As your guinea pig recovers from pneumonia you will need to keep him in a clean, stress-free environment so he can rest. Make sure you thoroughly clean and disinfect the guinea pig's cage before you return him to it and keep him separated from other guinea pigs to avoid spreading the disease. Maintaining proper sanitation of your cage environment will be the best way to prevent pneumonia from ever becoming a problem. Remove soiled bedding promptly from the cage and change out the bedding completely at least once a week. Keeping the cage clean is especially important if you keep more than one guinea pig in it because pneumonia can spread quickly.

Ringworm
Ringworm is a very common disease in guinea pigs and, despite its name, it is not actually caused by a worm. This condition is caused by a microsporum species of fungus, usually *Trichophyton metagrophytes*. Ringworm is fairly easy to identify because it results in round, ring-like bald patches on the guinea pig's skin. These patches typically appear first on the head, particularly on the face near the eyes and nose – from there, it can spread along

the back. Guinea pigs can transmit ringworm to other guinea pigs and the condition can also be spread through contaminated bedding and cage accessories.

The main cause of ringworm is the *Trichophyton metagrophytes* fungus, though other microsporum species can contribute as well. The most common sign of ringworm in guinea pigs is bald patches of dry, irritated skin. These patches may exhibit a crusty, flaky appearance, sometimes with red patches inside them. A visual examination of these patches is usually enough for a veterinarian to make a diagnosis of ringworm in guinea pigs. Your vet may also use an ultraviolet light to show the extent of the skin infection – skin scrapings may also be taken for laboratory analysis to confirm the diagnosis.

In some cases, ringworm goes away on its own. If it does not, it may require a 5- to 6-week treatment course of antifungal medications. When there are only one or two patches, or if the infection seems mild, your veterinarian may simply recommend an antifungal topical ointment. This type of treatment generally only lasts about 7 to 10 days and it is important that you finish the entire course of treatment. If the infection is severe and your guinea pig exhibits many patches of infection, you may need to put him on oral antifungal medications for 4 to 6 weeks.

Ringworm is highly infectious so you will need to separate the infected guinea pig from others while he is recovering. If all of your guinea pigs show signs of infection, however, you can keep them together and treat them all at the same time. You will need to thoroughly clean and sanitize the cage before placing your guinea pig back in it and maintain a high degree of sanitation throughout the course of treatment. Follow your veterinarian's treatment instructions closely and do not stop treatment early for any reason – if you do, the infection might come back. Always wash your hands after handling your guinea pig, especially before handling an un-infected guinea pig or anything from the cage. After you finish your guinea pig's course of treatment you should

93

go back to the vet for a follow-up to make sure the infection is completely gone.

Scurvy
Unlike rabbits, guinea pigs are not able to manufacture their own Vitamin C. For this reason, they must get adequate Vitamin C levels from their diet to prevent nutritional deficiencies. A deficiency in Vitamin C leads to a condition called scurvy. Scurvy may interfere with your guinea pig's body's ability to produce collagen, which is an important factor in healthy bone and tissue formation. Inadequate collagen production can also lead to blood clotting issues, joint problems, and skin problems. Unfortunately, vitamin C deficiency (scurvy) is fairly common in guinea pigs kept in captivity.

In most cases, scurvy develops in guinea pigs that do not get enough Vitamin C in their diets. In some cases, however, a deficiency may develop even when the guinea pig gets adequate Vitamin C from his diet. In cases like this, scurvy could be the result of a physical problem that keeps the guinea pig from eating enough or from some other factor that interferes with the body's ability to absorb the vitamin.

The most common symptoms of scurvy in guinea pigs include weakness, lack of energy, swollen joints, difficulty walking, bleeding under the skin, problems with blood clotting, rough coat condition, loss of appetite, weight loss, and diarrhea. If left untreated, scurvy can also result in sudden death. In order to make a diagnosis of scurvy, your veterinarian will take a thorough history of your guinea pig's diet and health. An initial diagnosis can be made by analyzing the guinea pig's diet and through performing a physical examination to look for joint or skin problems. Confirmation can be made through blood tests to check for Vitamin C levels.

In most cases, treatment for scurvy involves giving your guinea pig vitamin C supplements for one to two weeks. These supplements can be given by mouth, added to your guinea pig's water, or given by injection at the vet's office. It is not recommended that you give your guinea pig a multivitamin because guinea pigs sometimes develop allergic reactions to other minerals in the multivitamin.

As your guinea pig recovers from scurvy you will need to monitor his condition closely – you may also need to feed him a specialized diet as recommended by your veterinarian. Treatment for scurvy doesn't just involve treating the current problem – it also focuses on making sure the problem doesn't recur in the future. To help prevent scurvy in the future you should add some Vitamin C-rich foods to your guinea pig's diet like kale, bell peppers, tomatoes, broccoli, spinach, cabbage, oranges, and dandelion greens. Ideally, your guinea pig should be getting about 10mg of Vitamin C per day – pregnant guinea pigs need closer to 30mg per day of this vitamin.

Swollen Lymph Nodes
In guinea pigs, swollen lymph nodes are often caused by a bacterial infection – the bacteria most commonly responsible is *Streptococcus zooepidemicus*. This condition is characterized by inflammation and swelling of the lymph nodes – lymph nodes are found throughout the body but are most accessible in the head, neck and limbs. The lymph nodes play a role in distributing white blood cells throughout the body to combat harmful pathogens and dangerous foreign bodies. Swollen lymph nodes is often referred to as lymphadenitis and it is a condition that requires immediate veterinary care.

Some of the most common symptoms of lymphadenitis are swollen lymph nodes, pus-filled abscesses, head tilting, sinus inflammation, inflammation of the eyes, arthritis, difficulty breathing, pale skin, blueish skin, bloody urine, stillbirth, and fever. Though the *Streptococcus zooepidemicus* bacteria is the primary cause of lymphadenitis in guinea pigs, secondary contributing factors include irritating food, dirty bedding, overgrown teeth, and improper teeth alignment resulting in an inability to close the jaws. Guinea pigs can spread this disease to others by coughing, sneezing, genital contact, or cuts and scrapes in the mouth.

In order to make a diagnosis of lymphadenitis, your veterinarian will conduct a thorough physical examination. Additionally, he may take a fluid sample from the swollen lymph nodes to identify the causative bacteria. Your vet might also take blood or urine samples to test for increased white blood cell activity or protein in the urine. Treatment options for lymphadenitis may vary depending on the severity of the infection.

Unfortunately, antibiotic medications may not be enough to eliminate a lymphadenitis infection. In cases where pus-filled abscesses are present, treatment may involve opening and draining the abscesses. In some cases this may cause the bacteria to enter the guinea pig's blood stream, which may lead to an even more severe infection. Your veterinarian needs to be very careful about which treatment option he chooses. Even antibiotics can be dangerous for small animals like guinea pigs so they should be prescribed with caution.

As your guinea pig recovers from lymphadenitis you need to keep him in a clean and stress-free environment. Clean and sanitize your guinea pig's cage before placing him back in it and keep it as clean as possible. If your guinea pig has an abscess drained you will need to clean and dress the wound according to your vet's instructions. Always follow treatment instructions closely to ensure a fast and complete recovery for your guinea pig.

Urinary Problems
Guinea pigs are prone to developing a number of urinary problems including bladder stones and urinary tract infections. Bladder stones are not only a very painful condition for your guinea pig but they can actually be life threatening as well. Bladder stones are actually called uroliths and they are the result of crystallization of minerals and proteins in the urine in your guinea pig's bladder. These stones can be very small, small enough to be passed through the urethra. In most cases, however,

the stones are big enough that the get caught in the opening. When this happens it causes the tissue to become irritated and it may also lead to bleeding. If the stone cannot be passed it could lead to toxicity.

Some of the most common signs that your guinea pig has bladder stones include bloody urine, straining to urinate, malodorus urine, wet fur on the rear, swollen abdomen, hunched stance, excessive grooming of the rear, depression, loss of appetite, and weight loss. If your guinea pig doesn't get treatment for bladder stones it could lead to some very severe complications, even organ failure and death. In order to make a diagnosis of bladder stones, your veterinarian will need to take a thorough history of your guinea pig's health and diet. Blood tests and urinalysis may also help to confirm the diagnosis.

In some cases, bladder stones will pass on their own. If the stone is too large to be passed naturally, however, your vet might need to place a catheter through the urethra to allow the guinea pig to pass urine. In some cases the urolith can be removed surgically. As your guinea pig recovers, you should keep him in a clean and stress-free environment. Your vet may also prescribe certain antibiotics to prevent infection as well as various anti-inflammatories and pain medications.

Urinary tract infections are another urinary problem known to affect guinea pigs. Because the guinea pig has such short legs, the underside of its body often drags on the ground, where it can pick up pathogenic bacteria that might enter the urinary tract. Some of the most common symptoms of urinary tract infection in guinea pigs include bloody urine and painful urination. In order to diagnose your guinea pig with a UTI, your veterinarian will perform a differential diagnosis to rule out other conditions like pyometra, bladder stones, spinal injury, and interstitial cystitis. An x-ray may be required to rule out bladder stones and blood or urine tests might be taken to confirm the diagnosis.

Fortunately, urinary tract infections are fairly easy to treat with safe antibiotics like Bactrim. Your veterinarian may recommend a 1- to 2-week course of treatment, so make sure you follow out the entire course of treatment as recommended. Prevention options for urinary tract infections include keeping the guinea pig's cage clean and dry – trimming the hairs around the guinea pig's rump may also help to prevent infection. If your guinea pig suffers from recurring urinary tract infections adding some unsweetened, watered-down cranberry juice to his diet might help.

2. Preventing Illness

As you have already learned, providing your Teddy guinea pig with a healthy diet is the key to ensuring his health and wellbeing. Proper cage maintenance is also important for your guinea pig's health. If your guinea pig isn't kept in clean, sanitary conditions he may become stressed, which will increase his susceptibility to disease – it might also expose him to pathogenic bacteria or parasites that thrive in unclean conditions. It is important to remember that an ounce of prevention is worth a pound of cure – this simply means that it is easier (and better for your guinea pig) to prevent disease from happening than to try to treat it if it does.

In order to be a responsible guinea pig owner, you should learn to identify common signs of disease in guinea pigs. If you recognize one of these signs in your guinea pig you should take him to the veterinarian for diagnosis and treatment:

- Loss of appetite, refusing to eat
- Refusing to drink
- Labored breathing, wheezing, coughing
- Sneezing with crusty eyes, nose discharge
- Puffed-up coat, poor coat condition
- Dull eyes or receding eyes
- Lethargic or sluggish behavior
- Excessive drooling
- Water diarrhea, abnormal stools

- Blood in the urine
- Limping or difficulty moving
- Excessive scratching, patches of hair loss
- Loss of balance or coordination
- Unusual behavior

In addition to keeping an eye out for common signs of illness, you might also want to get into the habit of weighing your guinea pig on a weekly basis. For young guinea pigs that haven't yet reached full size you should expect a steady growth in weight. If an adult guinea pig loses two or three ounces it could mean that an illness is coming on – a loss of four ounces or more requires immediate veterinary attention. When you take your guinea pig to the vet make sure he knows that certain antibiotics like penicillins are deadly to guinea pigs – as long as the veterinarian is trained in guinea pig care, he should already know that.

Below you will find a list of medications that are considered safe for guinea pigs:

- Anigene shampoo
- Bimectin
- Panacur
- Calpol
- Daktarin foot cream/spray
- Canesten
- Brolene
- E45
- Sudafed
- Sudocrem
- Gripe water
- Kaolin
- Buscopan
- Cystitis sachets
- Dioralyte
- Probiotics
- Imaverol

- Glucose powder
- Vaseline
- Metatone
- Johnson's anti-mite spray

Not only do you need to prepare yourself just in case your guinea pig gets sick, but you should also be prepared in case he gets injured. You should consider putting together a first aid kit for your guinea pig and keep it near the cage – you should also take it with you if you transport your guinea pig somewhere.

Below you will find a list of items to include in your first aid kit:

- Critical care formula
- Probiotics
- Talc
- Bimectin – kills mites and lice
- Imaverol – fungal infection dip
- Lice shampoo
- Antiseptic cream
- Daktarin cream – for ringworm/fungal infection
- Fungal spray
- Trimmex/styptic powder
- Vitamin C drops
- Calcium supplement
- Metatone – to stimulate appetite
- Wormer
- Nail clippers
- Tweezers
- Syringes
- Mite shampoo
- Cotton pads/gauze
- Eye drops
- E-collar

3. Pet Insurance for Guinea Pigs

Taking your guinea pig to the vet can be expensive, especially since you will probably have to take him to an exotics veterinarian. To help mitigate your veterinary costs, you might want to consider purchasing a pet insurance policy. Pet insurance does for pets what health insurance does for humans – it helps to offset the cost of medical/veterinary services. The important thing to remember about pet insurance, however, is that the plan will not pay the provider directly (like health insurance plans do) – instead you will have to cover the cost upfront and then the plan will reimburse you at a predetermined rate up to 90% for most plans.

The details of pet insurance plans vary from one provider to the next and even within the same company. In exchange for coverage you will be required to pay a monthly fee called a premium- you may also have to pay a predetermined amount per year or per incident called a deductible before the plan will pay any benefits. It is also important to note that most pet insurance plans do not cover pre-existing conditions so you cannot purchase a policy if your guinea pig is already sick.

There are pros and cons associated with pet insurance and it might be a good option for some guinea pig owners but not for others. If your guinea pig gets sick a lot, having a pet insurance plan might significantly reduce your costs. If your guinea pig remains healthy, however, you might end up paying your monthly premium without ever really using your benefits. Before you buy a pet insurance policy, go over the details to make sure that you will be covered for the services you intend to use. You should also compare costs between different companies to make sure you get the best deal possible.

Chapter 9) Showing Your Teddy Guinea Pig

Showing your guinea pig is not a decision you should make lightly because it requires a great deal of time and preparation. Not only do you need to learn the requirements for showing guinea pigs at different shows, but you also need to familiarize yourself with the Teddy guinea pig breed standard as set by the ARBA. In this chapter you will find detailed information about showing guinea pigs in general as well as information specifically pertaining to the Teddy guinea pig breed. The information in this chapter will help you to decide whether showing your guinea pig is a challenge you would like to take on and, if it is, it will help you get started.

1. Teddy Guinea Pig Breed Standard

Before you even think about showing your Teddy guinea pig you need to make sure that he adheres to the breed standards set forth by the ARBA. These standards are what the guinea pig will be judged against with points being awarded in different categories. The breed standard also defines what characteristics are considered faults or disqualifications – if your guinea pig exhibits any of these characteristics you should consider not showing him. The Teddy guinea pig can be shown in six different categories divided by color and pattern. These categories include the following:

- Self
- Agouti
- Solid
- Broken Color
- Tortoise Shell & White
- Any Other Marked

Below you will find a list of general guidelines for showing Teddy guinea pigs as well as a breakdown of points used for judging them:

- The Teddy guinea pig should exhibit a medium body length with broad shoulders.
- The breed should have a Roman nose as well as a high, full crown.
- There should be no ridges or rosettes in the coat and the hair should be even over the entire body.
- The hair should be dense and naturally springy – it should demonstrate resiliency when touched

Breakdown of Points

Below you will find a list of categories for the Teddy guinea pig breed standard as well as a total number of points for each category, which all add up to 100:

Type (20 points)
Teddy guinea pigs should have a medium body length with broad shoulders, a Roman nose, and a high full crown.

Ears (5 points)
The ears should be shapely and slightly drooping, matching the variety description.

Eyes (5 points)
The eyes should be large, full and bright, matching the variety description.

Coat (45 Points)
Points are broken down as follows – Density 15 points, Length 10 points, Resiliency 15 points, Kink 5 points. The coat of the Teddy guinea pig should be close, thick and short as well as uniform in length. The texture is resilient and the hair shafts are kinky. The ideal length for the coat is about ¾ inch and softer coats are allowed in juniors. The coat should demonstrate resiliency when touched with the palm of the hand and it should be harsh and plush.

Color (15 points)

Teddy guinea pigs can be shown in six classifications: self, agouti, solid, broken color, tortoise shell and white, and other marked (including Dutch, Dalmatian, and Himalayan). Points are divided half between color quality and markings.

Condition (10 points)
Should be firm and fit, good size appropriate for age; body is short, cobby and thickset; wide across the shoulders.

Disqualifications – ridges, rosettes, parts of rosettes, or side whiskers; satin sheen; any suggestion of frontal hair.

Specific Faults/Penalties – feathering in the coat; coat too harsh or thin; coat over 1 inch long.

The Teddy Satin is judged with slightly different requirements than the standard Teddy. The main categories are type, coat, color, and condition. The type, color and condition are very similar to the standard Teddy but the breakdown of points within the Coat category is slightly different. You will find a breakdown of points below:

Breakdown of Points in the Coat Category

Coat (Total of 55 Points)
- **Sheen (15 points)** – The shafts of the hairs should reflect light, giving the coat a glowing sheen.
- **Density (12 points)** – The coat should be short and dense, standing out from the body.
- **Length (10 points)** – The coat should be even in length.
- **Resiliency (12 points)** – The coat should be luxurious and resilient, demonstrating resiliency when touched by hand.
- **Kink (6 points)** – The coat should be very kinky, standing out from the body.

2. General Tips for Showing Guinea Pigs

When it comes to guinea pig shows, each show will be a little different depending on the governing body that sponsors the show. In many cases, guinea pigs are shown in two different categories – purebred and pets. Purebred guinea pigs are those that belong to a recognized breed – like the Teddy – while pets are those of no particular breed. For purebred shows, animals are judged according to their breed standard, which identifies the ideal characteristics exhibited by the breed and tells the breeder how to present the animal for judging. Purebred guinea pigs are judged based on a number of physical characteristics including coat, body, and presentation.

Purebred guinea pigs are divided into three classes by age and weight. The following three classifications are used to categorize purebred guinea pigs for show:

Junior Boars and Sows – Up to 4 months of age; weight between 12 and 22 ounces.

Intermediate Boars and Sows – Up to 6 months of age; weight between 22 and 32 ounces.

Senior Boars and Sows – Over 6 months of age; weight over 32 ounces.

Guinea pigs being shown in the purebred category must also meet certain requirements in terms of condition and there are several faults and disqualifications that apply to all breeds. Below you will find an overview of the requirements for condition as well as a list of general faults and disqualifications:

Condition Requirements – Guinea pig should have a definite appearance of vigor and health with bold, bright eyes. The coat should be clean, full, and free of mats. The body should be firm, neither too fat nor too thin.

General Faults – Faults that apply to all purebred guinea pigs are those that detract from the animal's general appearance.

- Narrow shoulders or mid-section
- Bony or protruding hips
- Pinched hindquarters
- Flattened or squared hip/rump
- Shedding or coat out of condition
- Urine stains
- Broken toenails
- Poor ear carriage
- Too fat or too thin
- Stray colored hairs (all varieties)
- Skin tags or torn/slit ears

General Disqualifications – Disqualifications apply to all breeds and result in the animal being ineligible for show.

- Entered into the wrong class by sex, breed, or variety.
- Under or overweight for the class entered.
- Lack of permanent identification in left ear tattoo.
- Any signs of disease or hair loss.
- Heavy infestation of parasites.
- Any physical deformities.
- Patches of foreign hair color (consisting of 6 or more hairs) in all color varieties.
- Rosettes or partial rosette in American, American Satin, Coronet, Silkie, Silkie Satin, Teddy, Teddy Satin, Texel or White Crested breeds.
- Displaying vicious or uncontrollable aggression.
- Any faking to alter the natural appearance or condition.

Guinea pigs in the pet classification are usually hybrids of various purebreds so they must be judged to different standards. Judges for the pet classification do not look for a particular coat color or type. Instead, the guinea pig is judged for its cleanliness, its general condition, and its temperament. Purebred guinea pigs can be shown in the pet class, though they are usually the kind that do not quite stand up to the level of the show standard. Guinea pigs in the pet category can be any color or pattern – they can also have any length or type of coat as long as it is clean.

If you are new to the guinea pig show circuit, you may want to start off by showing your Teddy in the pet category – this will help you to learn the ropes of guinea pig shows.

When showing in the pet category, your guinea pig must meet the following three requirements:

1. The guinea pig must be clean; areas to be cleaned include the coat, grease spot, feet, ears, and nails. The nails should be trimmed to an appropriate length, the coat brushed to remove loose hair and free from knots; longhaired breeds are typically shown clipped.

2. The guinea pig should be in good overall health and sound condition, free from disease. The body should be well-fleshed and muscled, not fat, with a healthy coat and bright eyes.

3. The guinea pig should be tame, used to being handled, and exhibit a friendly and calm demeanor. Allowances can be made for young guinea pigs being more skittish.

The requirements for purebred guinea pigs are very similar, with details that vary according to each breed standard.

3. Grooming Your Guinea Pig for Show

In addition to familiarizing yourself with the Teddy breed standard, you also need to learn how to groom your guinea pig for show. Because the Teddy guinea pig has short fur you do not need to worry about trimming or wrapping it but you should still bathe your guinea pig to make sure he looks his best.

Below you will find an overview of the different aspects involved in grooming your Teddy guinea pig for show:

Bathing
The first thing you should do to prepare your Teddy guinea pig's coat for show is to bathe him. You should bathe your guinea pig about one week before the show for short coats and two weeks before the show for rough-coated breeds. Giving your guinea pig a bath will give his coat a nice shine because it stimulates oil production that will be worked into the hair over the next few days. When bathing your guinea pig you should fill a sink with a few inches of warm water and use a special shampoo designed for small pets.

Dipping
After bathing your guinea pig, you need to give him a flea dip to keep him flea-free for the show. Dip your guinea pig about one week before the show to kill any lice or lice eggs he may be carrying. Ask your veterinarian for recommendations on a flea dip product and follow the instructions carefully to ensure your guinea pig's safety.

Nail Clipping
Clipping your guinea pig's nails is very important because if you let them grow too long they will start to curl and could grow into the footpad. You should keep your guinea pig's nails short and neat, clipping them every few weeks to maintain a healthy length.

Be sure to use nail clippers specially designed for animals and avoid cutting the nail too short or you could sever the quick (the blood vessel that supplies blood to the nail), which will hurt your guinea pig and cause profuse bleeding.

De-Greasing
The guinea pig has a grease gland in its rump located where the tail would be. Male guinea pigs excrete a sticky substance from their grease glands when they are courting females or fighting other males for dominance. Before you show your guinea pig, you must make sure to clean this area using a cotton ball with some Dawn dish soap or coconut oil.

Chapter 10) Teddy Guinea Pig Care Sheet

Throughout this book you have been given information not only about Teddy guinea pigs, but about caring for guinea pigs in general. Before you decide whether the Teddy guinea pig is the right pet for you, you need to learn as much about them as you can. By the time you finish this book you should have a thorough understanding of what the Teddy guinea pig is like and how to care for guinea pigs as pets. When it comes time for you to bring your own Teddy guinea pig home, you may have questions about specific aspects of guinea pig care. Rather than rereading the entire book to find the answers to your questions you can simply refer to the guinea pig care sheet in this chapter. Here you will find an overview of the most important facts about guinea pigs and their care for quick reference.

1. Basic Breed Information

Scientific Name: *Cavia porcellus*
Breed Name: Teddy
Size: 1.5 to 2.5 lbs. (700 to 1,200g)
Length: 8 to 10 inches (20 to 25 cm)
Lifespan: 4 to 5 years on average
Coat Maintenance: high
Coat Length: short, even length throughout
Coat Texture: dense, kinky and springy
Coat Formation: even length all over the body; stands out from the body
Rosettes: none
Coat Color: wide variety of patterns and colors accepted; self, agouti, solid, broken color, tortoise shell and white, any marked
Temperament: curious, friendly, alert, amenable to handling
Health: generally healthy; may be susceptible to diarrhea, scurvy, parasites, and respiratory tract infections
Diet: fresh grass hay and food pellets; fresh vegetables, fresh fruit on occasion; fresh water daily

2. Cage Set-up Guide

Cage Size Minimum: 40 inches long by 20 inches wide by 20 inches high (102x51x51 cm)
Ideal Size (1): about 30-by-36 inches (76x91 cm); about 7.5 square feet (2.3m) of space
Ideal Size (2): about 30-by-50 inches (76x127 cm); about 10.5 square feet (3.2m) of space
Ideal Size (3): about 30-by-62 inches (76x157 cm); about 13 square feet (4m) of space
Ideal Size (4): about 30-by-76 inches (76x193 cm); minimum of 13 square feet (4m) of space
Cage Material Requirements: smooth material substantially impervious to liquids and moisture
Best Materials: plastic bottom with wire mesh sides
Materials to Avoid: wood, glass tank, acrylic tank, wire-bottomed cages
Location Factors: light, temperature, humidity, proximity to people and activity
Light: room that is brightly lit by indirect sunlight or by a window that gets morning light
Temperature: ideal temperature range between 65°F and 75°F (18°C to 24°C); never below 60°F (15.5°C) or above 85°F (29°C)
Humidity: low, stable humidity level; avoid showers, laundry room, and finished basements; also avoid drafty areas
Proximity: ideal location is near some family activity like the kitchen or family room
Indoors vs. Outdoors: indoors is ideal; outdoors only if climate matches temperature requirements
Types of Cages: glass/acrylic aquarium, pet store cage, outdoor hutch, cubes and coroplast, other
Recommended Accessories: food bowl, water bottle, chew toys, and shelter

3. Nutritional Information

Diet Type: herbivore
Nutritional Needs: 18% to 20% protein, 10% to 16% fiber, unlimited fresh water
Important Vitamins: Vitamin C, Vitamin A
Staple Diet: commercial hay pellets; avoid colorful mixes with lots of seeds
Supplemental Diet: unlimited fresh hay; 1/2 cup veggies per day; small amount of fruit twice per week
Feeding Amount: 1/4 to 1/2 cup pellets daily
High Vitamin C Foods: bell peppers, broccoli, kale, kiwi fruit, mustard greens, oranges, parsley, spring greens
Hay Types: alfalfa, botanical, oat, orchard, timothy
Nutritional Supplements: Vitamin C drops if needed
Alfalfa Hay: high in protein; good for pregnant, nursing guinea pigs and pups
Botanical Hay: blend of grasses and flowers
Oat Hay: thicker, good for grinding down teeth
Orchard Grass: soft; good for bedding
Timothy Hay: staple hay; favored by guinea pigs

4. Breeding Tips

Sexual Maturity: as early as 4 weeks, average 10 weeks
Female Breeding Age: 4 months or 500-600g (1.1 to 1.3 lbs.); not older than 12 months
Time Between Litters: recommended 3 to 4 months
Female Retirement: about 2 years; after 2 or 3 litters
Pregnancy/Delivery Complications: fairly common; toxemia, infection, blood loss
Sexing (Male): small slit above the anus, testes visible in adults
Sexing (Female): Y-shaped fold of skin above the anus, external urethral opening
Estrus Cycle: every 2 to 3 weeks; lasts 14 to 19 days
Female Receptive: for about 1/2 day per cycle
Receptive Behavior: female may arch her back and lift her hindquarters as the male approaches

Unreceptive Behavior: spray him with urine, lunge at him, or rear up and swat his face while showing her teeth

Gestation Period: about 65 to 70 days

Litter Size: average 2 to 4, possible up to 7

Before Labor: area between her pelvic bones will begin to dilate about 1 to 2 weeks before birth; maximum opening (2 fingers' width) occurs about 24 hours before birth

Labor: lasts about 10 to 30 minutes with 5 to 10 minutes between pups

Pups: born with fur, full set of teeth, open eyes, ready to run

Raising Pups: pups rely on mother for food and warmth for 14 to 21 days

Male Parent: male doesn't participate in raising the pups

Cannibalism: unlike many rodents, guinea pigs do not eat their young

Weaning: about 3 to 4 weeks of age

Separate Sexes: about 3 to 4 weeks of age

Chapter 11) Relevant Websites

Note: The websites mentioned in this book were active at the time of printing. However, by the time you read this book, the websites might no longer be active. That, of course, is out of my control as the Internet changes rapidly.

When you become a guinea pig owner you take on the responsibility of providing for your guinea pig's every need. Before you bring home your Teddy guinea pig you will need to purchase and set up his cage – you will also need to purchase food, toys, and various cage accessories.

The items you choose for your guinea pig are completely up to you but, in case you need some help finding them, you will find a list of relevant websites in this chapter. Here you will find a collection of resources to help you find the right food, cage, and cage accessories for your Teddy guinea pig. These resources are divided into United States websites and United Kingdom websites for your convenience.

1. Food for Teddy Guinea Pigs

The key to maintaining your Teddy guinea pig's health is to feed him a healthy, nutritious diet. In this section you will find a collection of relevant websites for purchasing food for your Teddy guinea pig.

United States Websites:

"Guinea Pig Food." Doctors Foster and Smith.
http://www.drsfostersmith.com/

"Guinea Pig Food." Pet Mountain.
http://www.petmountain.com/

"Vitakraft VitaNature Natural Guinea Pig Food." PetSmart.
www.PetSmart.com

"Oxbow Natural Science Adult Guinea Pig Food."
www.PetSmart.com

"Natural SunSations Guinea Pig Food."
www.SunSations.com

United Kingdom Websites:

"Small Pet Food." Pet-Supermarket.co.uk. www.pet-supermarket.co.uk/

"Guinea Pig Food and Treats." PetPlanet.co.uk.
www.petplanet.co.uk/

"Wagg Guinea Pig Crunch." Wagg.
www.waggfoods.com/

"Vitamin C Guinea Pig Food." Drs. Foster and Smith.
www.healthstory.co.uk/

"Small Pet Food." ZooPlus.co.uk.
www.zooplus.co.uk/

2. Cages for Teddy Guinea Pigs

Part of caring for your Teddy guinea pig involves providing him with a clean living environment. In this section you will find a collection of relevant websites for purchasing a cage for your Teddy guinea pig.

United States Websites:

"Cages and Pens." Doctors Foster and Smith.
www.drsfostersmith.com/

"Cages, Habitats and Hutches." PetSmart.
www.petsmart.com/

"C&C Cages." Guinea Pig Cages Store. http://www.guineapigcagesstore.com/

"Grid Wire Modular Shelving and Storage Cubes." Bed Bath and Beyond. www.bedbathandbeyond.com/

"Guinea Pig Cages and Habitats." Pet Mountain. www.petmountain.com/

"C&C DIY Guinea Pig Cages." PiggiePigPigs.com. www.piggiepigpigs.com/http://piggie

United Kingdom Websites:

"Guinea Pigs." CagesWorld.co.uk. www.cagesworld.co.uk/

"Guinea Pig Hutches." PetPlanet.co.uk. www.petplanet.co.uk/

"Hutches for Rabbit and Guinea Pig." ZooPlus.co.uk. www.zooplus.co.uk/

"C&C Cages." C&C Guinea Pig Cages. http://www.candcguineapigcages.co.uk/

"Safco Wire Shelving Unit." Wafair.co.uk. www.wayfair.co.uk/

"Ferplast Rabbit and Guinea Pig Cage 120." ZooPlus.co.uk. www.zooplus.co.uk/sho

3. Accessories for Teddy Guinea Pigs

In addition to purchasing a cage for your Teddy guinea pig you will also need to invest in certain accessories like food bowls, water bottles, toys, and shelters. In this section you will find a collection of relevant websites for purchasing cage accessories for your Teddy guinea pig.

United States Websites:

"Bedding and Litter." and "cage accessories" Doctors Foster and Smith.
http://www.drfostersmith.com

"Toys and Habitat Accessories." PetSmart.
http://www.petsmart.com

"Small Animal Toys." Petco.
www.petco.com/

"Guinea Pig Bedding and Litter."
www.petmountain.com

United Kingdom Websites:

"Guinea Pig Accessories." PetPlanet.co.uk.
www.petplanet.co.uk/

"Small Pet Bathing, Bedding and Nesting." Pet-Supermarket.co.uk.
www.pet-supermarket.co.uk/

"Cage Accessories." ZooPlus.co.uk.
www.zooplus.co.uk/

"Guinea Pig." PetShopBowl.
www.petshop.co.uk/http://www.pe
"Guinea Pig Bowls, Bottles and Accessories." Jollyes.
www.jollyes.co.uk/http://www.jollyes.c

"Small Pet Accessories." ZooPlus.co.uk.
www.zooplus.co.uk/

References

"A Brief Guide to Showing Guinea Pigs (Cavies)." British Cavy Council. http://www.britishcavycouncil.org.uk/Novice/ Showing/nov-showing-intro.shtml

"Animal Licensing." High Peak Borough Council. http://www.highpeak.gov.uk/hp/council-services/environmental-health/animal-licensing

"Animal Welfare Act." United States Department of Agriculture National Agricultural Library. http://awic.nal.usda.gov/ government-and-professional-resources/federal-laws/animal-welfare-act

Barbara Bean-Mellinger. "The Pros and Cons of Guinea Pigs as Pets." Mom.me. http://animals.mom.me/pros-cons-guinea-pigs-pets-7891.html

"Before Adopting a Guinea Pig." Jackie's Guinea Piggies. http://jackiesguineapiggies.com/beforeadoptingaguineapig.html

"Boarding Animals License." Bury Council. http://www.bury.gov.uk/index.aspx?articleid=3399

"Breeding and Babies." Pet Guinea Pig Care. http://petguineapigcare.com/breeding-babies/

"Breeding Info." Emma's Guinea Pigs. http://emmasguineapigs.blogspot.com/p/breeding-info.html

"Choosing a Guinea Pig." Jackie's Guinea Piggies. http://jackiesguineapiggies.com/choosingaguineapig.html#health

"Cost of Keeping Guinea Pigs." Think Animals. http://www.thinkanimals.com/guinea-pigs/cost-of-guinea-pigs

"Decorating Your Guinea Pig Cage." Guinea Pig Today. http://www.guineapigtoday.com/2011/12/21/decorating-your-guinea-pig-cage/

"Disorders and Diseases of Guinea Pigs." The Merck Manual Pet Health Edition. https://merckvetmanual.com/pethealth/exotic_pets/guinea_pigs/disorders_and_diseases_of_guinea_pigs.html

Erin Schimpf. "Guinea Pigs are Cheap...Not!" Guinea Pig Today. http://www.guineapigtoday.com/2011/11/24/guinea-pigs-are-cheap-not/

Fagnani, Stephanie. "How to Groom a Guinea Pig for a Show." Pets on Mom.me. http://animals.mom.me/groom-guinea-pig-show-7927.html

"Genetic Welfare Problems of Companion Animals." Universities Federation for Animal Welfare. http://www.ufaw.org.uk/LONGHAIRPERUVIANGUINEAPIG.php

"Guinea Pig Breed Types." Passion for Pets. http://www.passionforpets.com.au/dog-breeds/guinea-pig-breeds.aspx

"Guinea Pig Diet." Metropolitan Guinea Pig Rescue. http://mgpr.org/newsite/GP_Info/Guinea%20Pig%20Diet.htm

"Guinea Pig Glossary." Wheekly Reader. https://wheeklyreader.wordpress.com/tag/guinea-pig-terminology/

"Guinea Pig Glossary of Terms." Drs. Foster and Smith. http://www.drsfostersmith.com/pic/article.cfm?aid=2519
"Guinea Pig Health, Handling and Illness." K.L.C. Cavies. http://klccavies.weebly.com/guinea-pig-health-handling--illness.html

"Guinea Pig Housing." The Humane Society of the United States. http://www.humanesociety.org/animals/guinea_pigs/tips/guinea_pig_housing.html?referrer=https://www.google.com/

"Teddy Guinea Pig – A Quick Guide." Guinea Pig Hub. <http://www.guineapighub.com/teddy-guinea-pig.html>

"The American Guinea Pig: A Brief Guide." Online Guinea Pig Care. <http://www.onlineguineapigcare.com/american-guinea-pig-brief-guide/>

"USDA Regulations on Environment." Guinea Pig Cages. http://www.guineapigcages.com/USDA.htm

"Where to Put the Cage?" Guinea Pig Cages. http://www.guineapigcages.com/location.htm

"Which Guinea Pig is Right for You?" Guinea-Pig-Haven. http://guinea-pig-haven.webs.com/breeds.htm

"Wrapping a Peruvian Cavy for Show." YouTube. https://www.youtube.com/watch?v=EJmT0-mxp34

Index

121

Published by IMB Publishing 2015

Printed in Great Britain
by Amazon